DON'T LET OTHERS RENT SPACE IN YOUR HEAD

DON'T LET OTHERS RENT SPACE IN YOUR HEAD

*Your guide to living well,
overcoming obstacles, and
winning at everything in life*

GARY COXE

WILEY

John Wiley & Sons, Inc.

Published by John Wiley & Sons, Inc., Hoboken, New Jersey.
Published simultaneously in Canada.

For general information on our other products and services please contact our Customer Care Department within the United States at (800) 762-2974, outside the United States at (317) 572-3993 or fax (317) 572-4002.

Wiley also publishes its books in a variety of electronic formats. Some content that appears in print may not be available in electronic books. For more information about Wiley products, visit our web site at www.Wiley.com.

Library of Congress Cataloging-in-Publication Data:
Coxe, Gary, 1964-
    Don't let others rent space in your head / Gary Coxe.
      p. cm.
    ISBN-13: 978-0-471-74693-5 (cloth)
    ISBN-10: 0-471-74693-2 (cloth)
    1. Success in business. 2. Achievement motivation. 3. Expectation (Psychology) I. Title.
    HF5386.C885   2005
    650.1—dc22

2005019914

10 9 8 7 6 5 4 3 2

Special thanks to all those who believed in and stuck with me for so many years! And I would also like to thank those who motivated me by *not* believing in me.

To my father and mother, who supported me in everything I wanted to do. Even as a small child, I was never told that something wasn't possible.
Thanks for letting me dream and dream big!

Contents

Chapter 0

WHY MOTIVATION ISN'T ALWAYS MOTIVATIONAL   1

Chapter 1

WHAT DOES "DON'T LET OTHERS RENT SPACE IN
YOUR HEAD" REALLY MEAN?   13

Chapter 2

INQUIRING MINDS DON'T EVEN BELIEVE IT   23

Chapter 3

OKAY, YOU CAN RENT SPACE IN YOUR HEAD,
BUT ONLY TO GOOD TENANTS!   31

Chapter 4

YOU CAN'T CHANGE WHAT YOU
DON'T ACKNOWLEDGE   41

Chapter 5

WHEN LIFE GIVES YOU LEMONS, DON'T DRINK
THE LEMONADE   53

Chapter 6

IRRATIONAL OPTIMISM   59

Chapter 7

THE HOAX OF POSITIVE THINKING   73

Chapter 8

MENTAL VERTIGO—DO YOU HAVE IT?   93

Chapter 9

BEWARE OF THE MARATHON RUNNER WHO SMILES   103

Chapter 10

BE PREPARED TO ABORT OR LOSE AN ENGINE—
THE POWER OF NEGATIVE THINKING   111

Chapter 11

NOTHING IS GOOD OR BAD, BUT THINKING
MAKES IT SO!   131

Chapter 12

POSITIVE THINKING IS A LIE, BUT IT'S A START   147

Chapter 13

REWIRING YOUR BRAIN—GOING BEYOND POSITIVE
THINKING: THE FOUR-STEP PROCESS   161

Chapter 14

FEELING IS BELIEVING   191

Chapter 15

PLAY GAMES WITH YOUR MIND INSTEAD OF
LETTING YOUR MIND PLAY GAMES WITH YOU   213

Chapter 16

ACKNOWLEDGE THE JOURNEY   221

Chapter 17

IT'S TIME TO RE-EDIT YOUR VIDEO   229

Chapter 18

ENERGIZING YOUR LIFE IN SPITE OF THE
OBSTACLES—PULLING IT ALL TOGETHER   243

Chapter 19

"FILL YOUR OWN WELL SO YOUR CUP CAN RUN
OVER TO HELP OTHERS"   253

Index   *261*

WHY MOTIVATION ISN'T ALWAYS MOTIVATIONAL

WHY CHAPTER ZERO?

Most people don't read the introduction of books. I guess you should just think of this chapter as the introduction that I'm strongly encouraging everyone to read. This material will help you tune in to the attitude and objectives of the book, and it tells you how and why I wrote it. After reading this chapter, the body of the book will make more sense.

THE QUESTION

Every year, I talk to thousands of people. I regularly speak to audiences in convention centers and board rooms all across the globe, and my audiences come from every walk of life. Without exception, there is one burning question that I get more than any other. It's the one thing people tell me they most appreciate about what I teach. My life experience has lead me to answer the question in ways that no one else does, and in fact, my answers often fly in the face of conventional wisdom and contradict other experts. My answers to the question are the reason I wrote this book. And my answers have changed my life and the lives of many who have heard them. It's a great question, and I'm thrilled every time people ask it because it means that they are ready to experience some incredible truths about happiness, success, and the richness life has to offer.

Sometimes, people use slightly different language. Sometimes, they ask follow-up questions to explain their query more fully. But essentially the question is "In spite of life's obstacles, how do you keep going?"

That's not a simple question, and there are lots of answers too. I've dedicated my life to understanding the answers to that question and then sharing those answers with others.

In spite of life's obstacles, how do you keep going?

I am an avid aviation fan. I fly helicopters and airplanes, and I even hold a flight instructor's license (although I rarely have time to give lessons). When someone asks, "How do you fly a plane?" unless I have a lot of time, I usually give them this short answer: "You push the stick forward, and the houses get bigger; you pull the stick back, and the houses get smaller."

When I have time to give lessons to a close friend, I enjoy giving the long answer. I especially enjoy watching my friend progress, and I experience the thrill of learning to fly all over again with each new student pilot along the way. The short answer is cute and gets a laugh, but the longer answer is the one with all the true rewards. This book is a long answer.

The reason I have taken the time to write this book is because the sincerity and value of the question "How do you keep going?" deserves as thorough an answer as I can give. In these pages, we'll look at the question itself. We'll discuss some of the associated questions that cover topics like success, wealth, motivation, optimism, happiness, and positive thinking. But the real value in this book is the collection of real-world examples and tools you'll be given to keep yourself going and achieving for the rest of your life.

WORD PLAY ISN'T THE ANSWER

Too often, people are willing to accept answers from self-styled experts who are clever with language or say things that seem deep. In the course of my career, I have found that adults often listen better if you use clever language or stories to get a point across. Think about all the speakers who motivate or inspire you. Most of them use great stories or clever word play to capture your attention and to help you remember their points. Unfortunately, too many people who have mastered the media and who have a magnetic personality have nothing but clever answers that don't do much for us in the long run.

Now, don't get me wrong. I use stories too. They help people remember the points I'm trying to get across, and they make my points easier to understand. Anecdotes are a great training tool, but they aren't an end in themselves. It seems to me that simply making an observation about something and illustrating it with clever word play or a great story is the beginning and end for a lot of personal development experts. I see the need to go further. I always have tools or exercises to help people go beyond their current circumstances.

Unfortunately, too many people who have mastered the media and who have a magnetic personality have nothing but clever answers that don't do much for us in the long run.

I get some interesting feedback from people who hear me speak, because my goal is developing and delivering tools that help real people in actual situations, rather than simple motivation. Lots of public speakers love hearing praise after their events, and they are thrilled to hear that audiences are motivated. Although that seems like a terrific result and it shows everybody loved the speaker, getting motivated rarely helps people accomplish any more than they would otherwise. Ultimately, it doesn't do much more than provide a short-lived, warm, fuzzy feeling like you get from drinking a glass of wine. That's why I strive to look for tools that people can use to accomplish things once they feel motivated. Motivation is an important step along the way, but true progress comes from correct, consistent action, and motivation alone can lead to action, but not necessarily correct action. It's like pushing a parked car: You'll be active, but you won't be accomplishing anything.

I strive to look for tools that people can use to accomplish things once they feel motivated.

The tools you'll read about in this book are designed to get you moving and continuing in the right direction, and then keep you achieving for the rest of your life. The beauty of getting going and working with these tools is that the results will start a momentum. And the right momentum will automatically motivate you to keep going and achieving. Your life will become an automatic, self-improving cycle.

Keep in mind, though, that my tool kit is filled with dozens of useful tools, but every tool won't work in every situation. What's more, not every tool in the kit will even appeal to you. If you don't like a suggestion or particular tool, you don't have to use it. Different personalities approach obstacles and life problems (notice I didn't call them challenges, but we'll discuss that later) in different ways. What you will find is that most of the methods I teach work for most people.

Admittedly, I am an action-oriented personality. I have a drive to accomplish things (this book isn't just for people who are driven). But I was only inspired to tackle my current profession when I was slammed by life experiences that brought me down, and I found myself asking the question "How do I keep going?"

Initially, I reasoned that there had to be lots of people who had been there before me, so I looked to experts for insights. I found dozens of platitudes and a lot of clever word play but far too little substance that I could use to climb out of the place where life had dragged me. I had been dealt an incredible amount of tragedy in a very short time frame, and the typical solutions weren't sufficient for me.

One of the most annoying solutions suggested by friends and experts alike was to simply think positive. Some people think positive thinking feels good at first and seems to get you out of the really low places in life, but positive thinking was a lie, and it didn't help me at all. I was so far down that positive thinking was amplifying how bad I felt. What's more, people suggested that positive thinking was an end in itself and that was all I needed to do. That turned out to be as hollow as all the other answers people were giving. I think you'd agree, life's a bit more complicated than that. I still found myself asking, "Yeah, but how do I really keep going?"

One of the most annoying solutions suggested by friends and experts alike was to simply think positive.

I am where I am today because I had the good fortune to have a mix of very good and very bad experiences in my life, coupled with an interest in what drives people, and, of course, my faith. As an action-oriented personality, I was a true success story as a teenager. And when all that I had worked for was gone in a few short months, I didn't just ask, "How do I keep going?" I followed up with the question "And how did I get here in the first place?"

Unlike most people who have problems in their lives and work for years to get over their past, only to eventually chalk things up to a whole lot of bad luck and timing, I wanted to know more about the why. What was most frustrating to me was the fact that I would experience so many negative emotions in my life and I didn't know how to change them. And what was even worse was not being able to understand how I got them in the first place.

I didn't just want to know how to keep going, but I wanted to know everything about the experience so that I could master that situation and help others do the same. I came to the realization that it helps if you can identify how you came to feel a negative emotion. If this isn't done first, it's very difficult to change the emotions to something positive. What's worse than the negative emotions themselves is not knowing where they came from. At least if you know their source, you have somewhere to start.

What's worse than the negative emotions themselves is not knowing where they came from.

Think of this book as the result of my study of human behavior and a toolkit full of great strategies you can use to help you in your own life. In it, I'll show you how to play games with your mind instead of your mind playing games with you.

Interestingly, most people specifically avoid lingering too long on their bad experiences because that can be depressing. There is also some truth to the belief that whatever you focus on is what you will get out of life. Focusing on bad things can bring more bad things into your life. But I focused on my experiences, both good and bad, from a detached, clinical perspective so that I could work on mastering any circumstances life could throw at me. That's actually what many of my exercises help people do in order to master their own life.

WHEREVER YOU ARE, THAT'S WHERE
YOU NEED TO START

Later in the book, you'll discover that I have an action-oriented personality, and you'll find out how I have been beaten down by life's circumstances. That low point is where I started. This is *not* a book of ways to simply overcome depression brought on by life's circumstances, nor is it just a way to get rich or be successful, although it will help you with any of these ambitions or goals. There are tools in this book that can help anyone get to the next level, regardless of what that means.

There are tools in this book that can help anyone get to the next level, regardless of what that means.

ARE YOU READY TO ASK THE QUESTION?

More important, are you ready to take action when I tell you how to continue to keep going despite all obstacles?

Over the next few hours or days as you read this book, you will find yourself inspired and motivated. You will find your view of circumstances in your life will change. Then in a few more days, weeks, or months, you'll see that your life has improved, and you will have overcome problems that were keeping you back. You'll achieve more, feel better about yourself, and be more optimistic as you move forward. When you realize that your life is better, pick up this book again, and read it once more.

Two things will come from revisiting this text. First, you will reevaluate the tools you've used to get where you are, and you'll see that my suggestions are more than just words on a page and funny, memorable stories. This will crystallize in your own mind that these tools really do work and you should be willing to try more of these ideas. The other thing that will happen is that you will be in a new place in your life, and you'll be inspired to try new tools—or maybe try the tools that worked earlier, on new situations.

Again, this is where my approach is truly different from many others. Sometimes, books tell you to come back every year or two and read again, but most of the time their programs are based on rah-rah, pump-up motivation. They want you to get reenergized and reinspired. But remember, motivation is good and helps for a brief while, but it takes more than motivation to progress in life. It takes the proper mind-set and correct action to move forward and accomplish more. Because most motivational programs don't offer many usable tools, you need to just read the motivational stories again. What's worse, you need to wait a year or so to give yourself time to forget the stories so that they can reinspire you when you read them the second time.

When I ask you to come back, it's because I want you to see that the tools are working, and I want you to find new tools to apply to new situations. You may reread some stories that motivated you, made you think, or made you smile or cry, but that's not the main reason to come back. In fact, you'll find that the second time around, the stories do less motivating. It's the tools and your realizations about them that will help to keep you moving in the right direction.

Psychologists have identified a part of the brain responsible for increasing your awareness. It's called the reticular activating system. You know how it is when you buy a new car—all of a sudden cars just like yours start appearing everywhere! This book uses the reticular activating principle to help you build momentum. You'll use examples and tools from this book, and when you come back, you'll use your newly increased awareness to do even more.

Because my program is full of real, practical devices for helping real people to move to the next level in their life, the true motivation you'll experience will come from a different, better place. Your future inspiration should come from your successes (and perhaps some failures), not from my stories. And it will.

WHAT DO MOST PEOPLE WANT?

Usually, the question "how do you keep going?" is preceded or followed by a question about how to accomplish something, buy something, win someone's affection, or get past a bad experience. However you define success or whatever it is you want out of life, desires are essentially driven by certain needs we all have in common. Understanding these needs will help you to refine your personal goals and understand which tools will work best for your needs.

Most humans have several things in common. Considering that there are a few notable exceptions to these rules, usually associated with personality disorders, the following wants are shared by practically everyone. We want to be happy. We want to be healthy. We want to be loved by others. We want to have control of our own circumstances. We want to be successful. And to one degree or another, we want possessions. Usually, desired possessions point back to one of our other wants because many times we believe these things will make us happy or reflect our success, and although that may seem true to one degree or another, in the long run we need to resolve our wants differently.

Ultimately, to achieve our own definition of happiness, love, control, success, and health, we must truly master more than just obtaining the possessions we think we want. One of the real keys to happiness is to understand the entire process of personal achievement and all of the success components as well.

If you've read any book on success, time management, goal setting, increasing sales, or any topic remotely related to personal achievement, this truth isn't new to you. What's more, you have probably even read books or seen infomercials advertising programs that offer classes in how to reach some amazing level of personal happiness and success you only dream about.

> *One of the real keys to happiness is to understand the entire process of personal achievement and all of the success components as well.*

And if you've invested in a book or personal achievement program, you have already been exposed to a few of the ideas that most experts agree will help you reach your dreams (or your sales goals or whatever the desires of your heart truly are).

I think you'll find this book to be a little different in two important ways. First, you will be given many specific tools. You can expect detailed information that takes you well beyond what positive thinking proponents suggest. Ultimately, positive thinking is little more than a simple tool that doesn't even work unless you've laid an appropriate foundation to be ready for it, and then you have to know what to do after positive thinking.

And while I'm talking about positive thinking, let me just say this. When you hear some people talk, it seems as though the skills involved in positive thinking are relatively easy to master and that they can frequently make you feel good and overcome negative feelings in some situations. And because they make positive thinking sound so easy, it is an apparently attractive solution. Unfortunately, most positive thinking proponents offer little beyond this false hope. The truth is, depending on your situation, positive thinking and affirmations can make you feel even worse. There may be a time and a place for positive thinking, but it's not as useful as most people believe. This book will show you when it does and doesn't work.

> *Depending on your situation, positive thinking and affirmations can make you feel even worse.*

This book will take you well beyond positive thinking and give you a comprehensive collection of tools, each with its own specific role to play along your journey of personal achievement, success, and increased happiness. But, remember I said this book is different in two ways? Giving you a complete set of great tools and the necessary instructions to understand how they work and when to use them is only the first way this book is different.

The second way this book is different is that it is far more grounded in reality than others, and before you finish reading the last page, you'll understand that you will need to do some actual work to accomplish your goals. If that doesn't sound intimidating enough, maybe this will.

Although this book will help you to achieve your definition of success and happiness, the unfiltered truth is, bad things will still happen. You'll discover that the utopia promised by other self-help programs ignores the fact that life will continue to throw new obstacles in your path. No matter what you accomplish, you'll continue to ask, "How do I keep going?"

If you want a book that promises to make you feel good about yourself or human nature, you can find dozens of them. Unfortunately, they don't deliver real-world results, and any good feelings you may experience won't last. Just remember, motivation alone may feel good for a little while but rarely produces the results people rightfully demand in the long run.

There's a maturity in wanting to pursue life goals in spite of the work they require. If you've had enough of feel-good philosophies and you're finally ready to dig in your heels and accomplish your goals or whatever it takes to make your life worth living, and always keep moving forward, then turn the page and get ready for a life-changing experience!

Motivation alone may feel good for a little while but rarely produces the results people rightfully demand in the long run.

SUMMARY

▌ This book is about how to keep going in spite of problems and challenges.

▌ Clever sayings and stories are great if they help you remember something valuable, but too often experts try to motivate and inspire people with stories and clever words alone. You must go deeper.

▌ This book is a toolkit with ideas for overcoming obstacles and getting to the next level.

▌ Many popular answers are wrong and this book will dispel myths and help you understand truths behind human behavior.

▌ You need to understand the entire process of personal achievement in order to be able to truly achieve in your business and personal life.

▌ Depending on where you are in life, positive thinking may be counterproductive.

▌ Accomplishment requires work.

Chapter 1

WHAT DOES "DON'T LET OTHERS RENT SPACE IN YOUR HEAD" REALLY MEAN?

A big part of my life has been a study of the accomplishments of successful business people and of how they reached success. In the next chapter, you'll see how my motivations and strategies are considerably different from those of traditional life coaches and personal growth experts, and you'll start to understand why. (I don't even consider myself a life coach, but that's another story.) I've come to realize that people can accomplish more when they don't let other people or other things influence them in negative ways. I call this problem "renting space in your head." The concept of allowing others to influence decisions and behaviors is not foreign to anyone over the age of four. It happens all the time. Entire industries, like advertising, public relations, and financial advice are built on the principle of influence. Five-year-olds from time immemorial have practiced ways to influence their favorite grown-ups by exercising powerful forms of cuteness or by screaming like a banshee.

If you want to accomplish more and move to the next level in your life, your goal should be to be careful not only to avoid letting other *people* rent space in your head, but to also avoid letting other *things* and even *your own negative thoughts* take up valuable space. It's my experience that our own negative thoughts are often our own worst enemy. The more difficult we perceive our past to have been, the more we let negative perceptions control our very being. And they control our future. As humans, we have ideas, goals, relationships, and other concerns that we want to accomplish or pursue, but our future frequently gets smothered when we let something rent space in our head.

POWER TIP

Dreamers never sleep with their eyes closed.

It's my experience that our own negative thoughts are often our own worst enemy.

One of the techniques I use when starting a speaking engagement is to begin with a thought-provoking question: "Where would you be, what would you be doing, what would you have, and, more important, how would you think differently if you didn't let anyone, anything, or your own negative thoughts from your past, rent space in your head?" Consider that question yourself. And, by the way, if you're human, you *do* let things rent space in your head. That's just a part of being human. But the degree or the amount of space that you have available for rent depends entirely on you.

A corollary to this principle is the rule of risk taking. The rule goes like this: The more risk you take in life and in business, the greater tendency you have to let others rent space in your head. People have a natural tendency to want cues about how they should respond to new situations. If you are trying something extraordinarily new or unique and you're stretching well outside your comfort zone, you'll look for reinforcement about your behavior. People who are incredibly successful have mastered the ability not to let others rent space in their heads. They just want factual feedback about their risks, and they don't attach emotional meaning to it. Maybe you've already started to limit the space you allow for negative thoughts, but if you truly master this concept yourself, you won't just be able to think outside the box. You'll be able to consistently think way beyond it.

Consider this: Once you start down an unfamiliar path and take risks and look for feedback, your mind may let in negative thoughts, if your results aren't as grand as you've hoped. Keeping things from renting rent space in your head is a marathon that never ends.

Your mind may let in negative thoughts, if your results aren't as grand as you've hoped.

Roger Banister broke the four-minute mile because he refused to let negative thoughts cloud his thinking. The impossible four-minute mile didn't rent space in his head.

Imagine thinking so far outside the box that you're out of this world! That's exactly what Richard Branson has done. Branson is an incredibly gifted business man, founder and CEO of Virgin Airways and Virgin Records, and a billionaire adventurer. Recently, he purchased not one, not two, but *six* space planes. I even feel a little bit silly writing that down. Richard Branson bought six spaceships!

What do you think Richard Branson wants with six space

planes? He wants to take you to a hotel in space. Wouldn't you imagine that somebody who heard about Richard Branson's plans for space planes and zero-gravity hotel rooms would think he was whacked? Absolutely! But the truth is, commercial space travel is a reality, and Richard Branson is benefiting from it.

Do you think Richard Branson would have bought space planes or considered hotels in space if he had let others rent space in his head?

I'd like to introduce you to another forward-thinking person who doesn't allow people to rent space in his head. He's my business mentor, and I want to share a story about an amazing success he achieved because of the way he thinks.

Many years ago, he chose to enter the hotel business. He had absolutely no experience in the hotel industry, and that's just the beginning. The hotel property he bought was derelict and vacant. After the previous owner went out of business, it sat empty for some time.

Without even talking to the former owner, my mentor found a few clues as to why it had gone out of business. The property was literally a stone's throw away from the runway of an international airport. Jumbo jets and all kinds of commercial and private planes landed and took off all day long. The noise obviously disturbed the guests.

Needless to say, many people thought the property wasn't a good investment, especially for someone whose major business experience was selling air conditioners. My friend was getting into a business he knew nothing about, right across from a busy runway. People weren't shy, and several told this novice hotelier that his investment would never work. Some even thought he was crazy.

Put yourself in his shoes. Would you leave a business that you knew well and invest a huge amount of money (much of it borrowed) in a hotel that had failed before? What's more, it had remained empty long enough for other hotel managers to know about it, and they had passed on trying to rehab the property. Nobody wants to bet on a sure loser. If you look at it that way, the whole idea was scary.

Instead of allowing other people to rent space in his head, this businessman pushed forward. He invested in redesigning the hotel and making it presentable for guests. He stayed focused on his goal and turned negative thoughts into neutral statements that he could manage.

What about the noise? He didn't have the resources to close an international airport. Besides, even if he could have, he wouldn't have wanted to because travelers wouldn't be able to get to his beautiful resort easily. When you refuse to let other things and other people rent space in your head you think on a totally different level. Today, if you visit this first-class resort, you'll still see and hear loud jets taking off, yet the resort couldn't be more successful! Unless you've been there, you're probably wondering how this property could be a hit. What's absolutely amazing is that guests aren't even bothered by the noise.

When you refuse to let other things and other people rent space in your head you think on a totally different level.

Every guest arriving at this beautiful resort actually participates in an orientation. This policy allows each guest to immediately become familiar with all of the available restaurants, tours, activities, and amenities. That alone is thinking outside the box. Part of the orientation includes a story about the special tradition everyone joins in whenever jets depart. Everyone stops what they're doing and waves at the planes to wish the folks that are leaving a safe journey. The staff promises that when you leave everyone will do the same for you too. You can confirm this by looking down on the resort as you depart.

What's even more clever is that, because this is a romantic couples resort, the staff suggests that each couple should kiss one another right after they wave to seal the wish. In this way, the tradition becomes a romantic pastime rather than a noisy distraction. Brilliant!

IT'S CLEVER AND IT WORKS

Imagine that you are sitting at dinner with friends. Every five minutes or so, something noisy interrupts your conversation. Usually, this would be annoying. Yet at wedding receptions all across the country, there's a tradition of clinking glasses until the bride and groom kiss. It's loud and distracting, and if you were in the middle of a conversation, it would normally be annoying, but at the wedding reception everyone in the room is smiling and happy. It's a new way to think about noise. Without quite a bit of unique thinking in new ways and refusing to let others rent space in his head, my mentor's luxury couples resort would never have been successful, much less would it have launched a nationally recognized chain of resorts. His name is Gordon "Butch" Stewart, and you'll learn more about him later.

So let's assume you agree with my ideas. Here lies the challenge. How do you get to a point where you limit the amount of space that things rent in your head so that you can make phenomenal things happen in your own life? Read on, because that's the point of this book.

Maybe you can accept this new way of thinking logically, but you'll need to go further to internalize it. You need to adopt this new mindset *emotionally* as well as logically.

For example, I can't tell you how many times I've heard a sales manager speaking to someone new to sales and saying something like "It's just a numbers game. They say, 'the more people you talk to, the closer you are to the sale.'" *Duh!*

We can *all* understand that logically. But thoughts like this don't matter to people who have never been there—people who have never made a sale in the first place. They haven't made the emotional connec-tion because they don't have any positive

experiences (talking to enough people and eventually mak-ing sales) to build on. Telling new sales recruits that the more no's they get, the closer to a yes they are, is like telling some-one, "If you keep eating junk food, you're going to die. Well, *duh* again!

People may intellectually understand all this, but it takes more than a clever statement for it to click. One of my goals is to show you how to move forward and make monumen-tal leaps so that you can experience phenomenal personal and professional success, even *before* you've experienced the joys of a success on your intended path. What's more, I'll give you tools so you'll be able to recognize the steps you ought to take to develop your own logical plan of action.

From time to time, we all have doubts or insecurities, but there is something within incredibly successful people that helps them refuse to reward their negative thoughts. They simply don't let others rent space in their heads. This is one of the keys to their success.

There is something within incredibly successful people that helps them refuse to reward their negative thoughts.

One thing you'll need to be careful about is trying to create these mind-sets when you're at a low point in your life. The time to master this skill *isn't* when you're down and out. If you're low right now, don't put the book down and give up. There are all kinds of tools and strategies in this book, and some will help you get far enough up to change your attitude, so that you can employ this strategy.

Just so you know, I'm not talking about positive thinking. A few chapters from now, you'll start to see that I absolutely don't believe in traditional positive thinking. Positive thinking would tell us that we should say, "The more no's you get, the closer you are to a yes." As I have said, this advice works only for people who are ready to hear it, because they have experienced a positive result. If you're talking to people who don't believe a statement on an emotional level, you can give them advice until you're blue in the face, but they are going to fight you all the way. They'll hate the process, and any results won't last long.

So what about you? It's time to ask yourself that important question: "Where would you be, what would you be doing, what would you have, and how would you think differently if you didn't let anyone or anything (even your own thoughts or experiences) rent space in your head?"

And if you're intrigued, remember you have the control. Just turn the page. You're taking control of your journey.

SUMMARY

▌ People can accomplish more when they don't let other people or other things influence them in negative ways. I call the problem "renting space in your head."

▌ Both people and things can influence your behavior.

▌ People and things rent space in our heads because we are looking for feedback about what we're doing.

▌ If the results of our efforts seem less than perfect, it's natural to look for problems and let our negative interpretations influence us to react in negative ways.

▌ It's inevitable that some people and things will influence your thinking, so you must practice in order to recognize those things that influence you and to decide which things to evict from your sphere of influence—and which to keep.

- You can control your journey by controlling the things that influence your behavior.

Chapter 2

INQUIRING MINDS DON'T EVEN BELIEVE IT

UNDERSTANDING MY BACKGROUND

My life story isn't the purpose of this book, but it is important because it helps many people understand where I'm coming from. I have found that people use all kinds of excuses when I'm giving good, solid advice, and one of the biggest excuses is that "I personally don't know what it's like to be really down." The fact is, I do. And when you hear some of the unbelievable things I've been through, you may feel bad for me. Don't. I am able to look at my life clinically, and my experiences are all a part of who I am. I love my life, and I love having the chance to help other people master the problems and roadblocks in their lives. My past has allowed me to understand essential human truths and master my perceptions—to move on to the next level. I don't watch much television, but when I see what passes for drama on TV these days, it makes me laugh. I guess I had enough real-world drama in my own life so that the TV kind just doesn't do anything for me.

From a very early age, I knew I wanted to be in business. I was fascinated by the idea that I could create something that was valuable enough to other people that they would pay money for it. To a degree, playing and school were a regular part of my childhood, but my real excitement always came when I was doing something toward my business. I was just 11 when I noticed that people were carrying beaded key chains and they would buy just about anything made of macrame. (The '70s were memorable for more than just leisure suits.) I learned how to make macramé key chains, because I could make them quickly, and people were buying them almost as fast as I could make them. Before the key chain market dried up, I started looking for something a bit more unique, something that could generate even more profit. I discovered that I could carve black coral and create fine jewelry pieces that were even more profitable than the key chains. My entrepreneurial interests were only just beginning, but the rewards were great!

Playing and school were a regular part of my childhood, but my real excitement always came when I was doing something toward my business.

Keep in mind, this isn't a business book, and I'm not trying to teach you how to start and run a business, but I want you to have some insight to my personality. (By the way, there isn't much market for beaded key chains anymore.) I was, and I am, a driven, action-oriented person, and I loved business and the rewards that came from it. I was regularly making a profit that grown-ups would have envied, and I didn't know it was supposed to be hard. Unfortunately, I had a less than amicable relationship with my stepfather, and my ability to out-earn him seemed to create even further alienation.

I haven't yet used the term "Type-A personality." I have come to understand that people's perceptions of certain words or phrases can make them to believe or behave in certain ways. In my mind, the term "Type-A" has negative connotations, and these bad perceptions are part of the popular lexicon as well. Because some people already have a negative view of Type-A personalities, I don't want to say that's what I am. For example, I think of some Type-A people as being driven to the point where they lack balance in their lives. I may be driven. I may push harder than most people do in certain situations. But I have balance in my life, and I value my family and my spiritual life too.

I had a less than amicable relationship with my stepfather, and my ability to out-earn him seemed to create even further alienation.

I took my success with jewelry to the next level by adding jewelry repair to my business. Based on my ability to repair and even create jewelry, I started to sell new customized fine jewelry. I wasn't following in the family business or doing what a family mentor suggested. I just liked being in business, and the jewelry business came from a natural progression of my entrepreneurial experiences. I simply enjoyed being my family's first-generation jeweler.

When I was in high school, I entered the school's work experience program and tried to work for someone else part-time. That didn't work at all. (I am now certain exactly which side of the fast food counter I never want to see again.) Business thrilled me, but hourly grunt work didn't. The intellectual payoff wasn't there. I went back to my principal, and I negotiated a deal.

Most public schools receive a fixed amount of funding from the government according to the number of students who are enrolled. Whenever students leave or drop out, the school loses thousands of dollars. At the end of my junior year, I told my principal that I simply hated school and I planned to leave. I also told him that I knew he would lose funding if I did, so I suggested a compromise. I suggested that he allow me to work for myself full-time, and rather than spend any school resources on my curriculum and grades, I would grade myself, and ultimately earn my diploma and graduate with my classmates at the end of the year.

> *I suggested that he allow me to work for myself full-time, and rather than spend any school resources on my curriculum and grades, I would grade myself and graduate with my classmates at the end of the year.*

Without a single question or time to consider my proposal, he simply agreed. During my senior year, I never set foot on school grounds; I ran my business full-time; I earned my diploma; and, you'll be happy to know, I got a perfect 4.0 GPA.

Although nearly all high school seniors would love to grade themselves and never have to take a class, my business wasn't an excuse to get out of school. It was an enterprise. I even hired some of my classmates, and I was bringing in over $1,000 a week!

By society's standards, I was doing really well. I had a great sports car, a solid income, and a growing jewelry busi-

POWER TIP

Feelings change last.

ness. I was able to buy things lots of adults could only dream about owning, and I even married my high school girlfriend. I was proud of what I had accomplished, and things never looked better. In retrospect, I thought this game called life was pretty easily mastered, and I wasn't sure what all the fuss was about. Nothing had prepared me for what I was about to discover.

My wife got pregnant and eventually gave birth to a boy who had to be placed in intensive care for two weeks. I had never even been around anyone who needed hospital care, and my new boy's birth started a storm of emotions I was totally unprepared to handle. I was blessed and challenged, I was happy and scared. And above all, I was confused. I didn't know what to do or how to feel, but I probably could have handled this curve ball somehow. Then my wife confessed that the son I had loved since before he was born wasn't even mine. I was devastated. It felt as though somebody had pulled my heart out of my chest, the pain was so intense.

I was still confused and deeply emotional, but I felt that somehow I should start looking for a way to overcome this tragedy. I had only begun to come to grips with my situation and was still far from getting past the pain and confusion when my father was brutally murdered, my grandfather and stepfather died of cancer, and my uncle was killed in a plane crash. All this happened before I turned 21.

When this had all started, I had $30,000 in the bank. When I took stock of everything that had happened, I had lost family members, friends, all my money, and my $100,000 a year business. I was barely out of my teens, I was suicidal, and I seemed to have good reasons to be. In fact, I had to be hospitalized and put on medication for a time.

When this had all started, I had $30,000 in the bank. When I took stock of everything that had happened, I had lost family members, friends, all my money, and my $100,000 a year business.

My life was so incredibly bad that the *National Enquirer* even ran a full-page story about my success and tragedy. I know the reputation of the *National Enquirer* but I assure you, they did not have to invent anything in their story.

COMING BACK WAS A DIFFERENT PROCESS

As you've already guessed, I did eventually recover from my downward spiral, but it's important to understand that there was no specific ah-ha moment. There was no one thing I read or heard that helped me suddenly overcome my pain and start achieving again. In some ways, I was doing what you might expect. I was depressed, and I drank a lot. I had adopted a hermit's lifestyle and listened to depressing music that reinforced my negative outlook. I thought I needed time to absorb what had happened. But in a few key ways I was different too.

I had experienced terrific success early in life, and my passion for business had been rewarded. I had the memories of that success, and I found myself focusing on them to overcome my present dim view of things. I had managed to succeed in business once, so I decided to tackle it again.

I was able to succeed in business again in a relatively short time, but I must admit that achieving a measure of wealth once more was far easier than trying to be normal again. Business was natural enough for me so that success afforded me the time I needed to spend focusing on what makes people normal. I had a burning curiosity to discover how we function as humans, and more important, I needed to understand how I could bounce back as quickly as possible. After all of these tragedies, I was riddled with powerful psychological limitations: fear of failure, fear of success, fear of falling in love, fear of losing family—and the list goes on.

I was able to succeed in business again in a relatively short time, but I must admit that achieving a measure of wealth once more was far easier than trying to be normal again.

Again, no earth-moving revelations here. I just started making little improvements in my life. I opened the shades on my trailer to cast out the dark and let in the light, and then opened the windows to let in fresh air. I started to listen to more positive, upbeat music, and I realized that it was the little things that made the biggest difference for me. I kept studying my situation and comparing where I was to where I wanted to be. I rekindled my faith. I let friends know that I had opened my windows and changed my music, and that I was going to succeed after all. My friends and family were happy that I had reentered the world and that I was doing well in business again. I started hearing people ask, "Gary, how did you keep going?" It was then that I discovered the true pleasure of sharing my discoveries with others.

> **POWER TIP**
>
> When my feelings are not in harmony with my goals, ignore my feelings.

It was then that I discovered the true pleasure of sharing my discoveries with others.

TRADITIONAL SELF-HELP BOOKS JUST HELP THE AUTHOR

One of my revelations was that there wasn't much out there on how to keep going in spite of life's tragedies. To me, it seems that the positive thinking books crowding the shelves don't help anyone but the authors. Don't get me wrong. There's nothing wrong with writing a book to make money, but if the stated intent of the book is to help people and the techniques haven't been proven over time, or if they might just do more harm than good, that's when I have a problem. As for information that can help people overcome tragedy or simply move from a good place to a better one, I found very few practical answers. I honestly don't think many of the positive thinking proponents have ever done much more than read a few books and reword someone else's philosophy on optimism.

SUMMARY

▊ Just in case you think that I'm just a self-help expert with letters after his name—someone whose actual experience is limited to the post-graduate classroom—you're wrong.

▊ The personal tragedy I've experienced may be amazing, but I never use it as an excuse to give up.

Chapter 3

OKAY, YOU CAN RENT SPACE IN YOUR HEAD, BUT ONLY TO GOOD TENANTS!

Have you ever stopped to take the time to figure out why you act or think the way you do? To figure out the results or lack of results in your life? I mean, have you ever been able to identify a *specific* event that happened in your life, especially as a very young child, that influences your actions and personality to this very day?

We are essentially the product of everything that we have ever experienced in our lives, from birth to this very moment. Life experiences and relationships have greatly influenced our behaviors, thought processes, and many of our actions. Our lives have been a compilation of lessons learned from our culture, parents, grandparents, schooling, teachers, and religion—not to mention genetics. You can't change your genetics, so let's focus on the environmental influences, because those can be changed and updated.

Even when you wake up, you have a specific pattern you start with each day. It's usually the same one over and over and over. You've been engaged in it for years, and it has evolved from being a habit to being a ritual. It's almost as though you're on autopilot. There are things that each of us do every day because someone or something programmed us. A tremendous amount of this programming began when we were children.

I often try to identify why I think, act, and do what I do, and I try to see if I can remember specific experiences that cause me to respond in ways that I do.

Focus on the environmental influences, because those can be changed and updated.

For example, when I was 9 or 10 years old, I was spending the weekend with my grandparents. We were all sitting at the dinner table playing Monopoly. We got to a point where I was losing pretty badly. I was frustrated, and I threw my dice onto the board. I didn't launch them at anyone, and it wasn't a vicious throw, but it was obvious I was angry. I'll never forget what happened next. My grandfather immediately folded the board in half, put everything away, and said, "We don't play that way." I looked at him in astonishment. I was used to getting second chances at school, so I expected him to give me another chance. I thought he would just unpack the game and we'd start over. Not a chance. The rule was "we don't play that way." That's it. I'll never forget that. The lesson? Don't be a sore loser! A great lesson indeed.

Consider my grandfather's approach. He didn't pull the

new age parenting garbage and tell me we needed to talk about my feelings and about why I threw the dice. He didn't give me another chance and offer to keep playing if I would just promise not to throw the dice or have some other temper tantrum. If he had, what would have been my answer? I'd have promised not to misbehave, and I probably would have stuck to my promise for that day, and maybe even for the rest of the weekend, but I didn't get a second chance.

POWER TIP

Having a reason why you want to change isn't enough. It's the amount of value you have on the why that creates the determination to never give up.

I later realized he had taught me another lesson: Don't give in. Tough love has its place, and my grandfather's example has stuck with me to this day. Now, some readers will feel sorry for me (as a child) or that there might be a gentler way to get the same point across. Consider, though, that this was just a board game. Consider as well that if I had been given a second chance, I probably wouldn't have remembered the lesson this long.

I can see the incident in my mind's eye as if it happened yesterday. It's like a video I can run any time I want. I've played this video over and over. The video in my mind is no more than about five seconds. I get upset and throw the dice; my grandfather folds up the board game; and I hear, "We don't play that way."

We have all been programmed like this. It happened all the time when we were young, and it still happens, though somewhat less frequently and intensely, to adults. Programming has to do with survival behavior. We learn what it takes to get the results we want or need, and we remember lessons, both negative and positive. Ironically, we usually forget the core reason we develop certain thought patterns, and sometimes we don't even recognize the core belief that resulted from it.

We just react a certain way because of what we have learned or believe. The problem is that when we received the original programming, our ability to draw the *correct* conclusion may have been limited or inadequate.

As adults with an ever-growing collection of experiences, we should regularly review our beliefs (and original lessons if we can remember them) and see if the lessons are true and if the beliefs are helping us. If not, it's time to look for new lessons and experiences to replace the bad ones. As you'll learn later in this book, when you can identify a limiting belief and change it, you begin to get a new result immediately. It's an exciting realization, and that's the point of my book and my seminars.

It's time to look for new lessons and experiences to replace the bad ones.

Fortunately, I remember this story about my grandfather. I remember the video. I remember the lessons. I still hold the resulting beliefs. I am certain that I have many more positive lessons, but I don't recall their origin and couldn't find the video for the life of me.

On the other side of the coin are the negative programming experiences. (I guess when I was a child I might have considered that lesson a negative experience, but the negative is so small in proportion to my life and the positive so large that I consider it a positive memory.) As you can imagine, I have a tremendous amount of footage on file of negative lessons. Just as we allow positive experiences to program us, we certainly allow the negative ones to do the same.

The sad thing is that, in spite of the fact that we are a product of our experiences and lessons, we can't consciously remember a fraction of the experiences that are responsible for programming us. This means, unfortunately, that much of our programming has been subconscious or is played out in our behaviors subconsciously. Unless we take action to control our programming, we're like a kite. We're at the mercy of the direction and velocity of the wind.

If you want to master your circumstances and your life, there must come a time when you say, "Stop! This is all a choice. I can allow or not allow this negative or positive experience to affect my life, to *rent space in my head.*"

If you need just one more little reason to embrace change and squeeze more out of life, consider this. Life is empty when everything and everyone control you. Freedom of choice and freedom to succeed are enriching on so many levels, and the realization that these freedoms are a matter of choice can be incredibly empowering.

Caring for your mind is like owning real estate. Some people are great investors and landlords, while others are not. Good investors own quality properties with good tenants, and the value of their investments goes up. One of the keys to having good tenants in your portfolio is your prequalifying process. If you don't prequalify properly, you are going to have bad tenants. Then there are times when, no matter how well you prequalify, you may still have to evict people. The longer you wait to evict them, usually the more repairs and clean-up you are going to have. Putting off evicting bad tenants also damages your property and keeps you occupied with troubles and worries that waste your valuable time and money. If you realize that you need to prequalify your tenants and quickly evict the bad ones that slipped through, you'll be a successful investor. Master that concept, and it will yield great results.

Caring for your mind is like owning real estate. Some people are great investors and landlords, while others are not.

We all have space in our heads for rent. But we can choose our renters, good tenants or bad. Unfortunately, many people forget this lesson, while others don't even realize that they truly have a choice. As we discussed earlier, we have been subjected to an enormous amount of programming, especially while growing up, when we were too young or inexperienced to decode the associated choices. Then, as we get older, what has been ingrained in our minds manifests itself in the results we experience. As we grow older, we must realize that we need to be responsible for our own actions. This means that we should try to deprogram much of the junk and limited thought processes that so many of us are exposed to. The process takes time and can be a truly monumental effort, but the payoff is worth it.

If an investor purchases an occupied apartment building, he gets all the tenants that come with the building. They are probably not all great tenants. From a business perspective, what should the new owner do? He may have to evict some tenants, which takes time, money, and headaches. He may just wait until the tenant's lease is up and not renew it, with the hope of finding a better replacement.

I have to say that the large majority of adults today have buildings with bad tenants. You've heard the stories: "I've had a hard life, a terrible upbringing." "My mother or father or friend did this or that or treated me this or that way." You need to start by realizing that the experiences that caused you to believe and behave as you do are lessons that may have been misinterpreted, and they may be altogether wrong. Okay, what's next?

We need to go through each tenant lease in all of our mental property and make a conscious choice as to whom we are going to keep and who needs to be evicted. Remember, the longer you wait to evict, the more problems and expense you'll experience. Because we're talking about limiting ideas and beliefs and not causing someone's homelessness, and because there are no contracts forcing you to retain bad ideas (tenants), you should feel good about getting rid of the bad ones as soon as possible.

Essentially, your goal here is to allow helpful beliefs and ideas to remain in your mind while quickly dismissing (evicting) limiting or incorrect beliefs. (Notice that I didn't say to evict negative thoughts. That's because negative thoughts can be as powerful as positive thoughts if their influence provides desired outcomes. That's the whole point of Chapter 10.)

Don't worry if it's not apparent how to accomplish this right away. It's important for now that you just try to understand the fundamental principles.

I use a variation on this concept in running my business. When I'm involved in the interview process for management or upper-management candidates, I let them know that I never want to rent unnecessary space in my head. I tell them that they are most valuable to me if they don't rent space in my head as part of their day-to-day job. For example, if I delegate five projects or responsibilities ("balls") to them and they drop one, I am now thinking about that problem *plus* which other ball they might drop. My team understands that they get paid so that I don't have to think about their job. If employees start developing a track record of dropping the ball and renting too much space in my head (when I wonder if they've done their job), then there is a problem. If the problem persists, there's an eviction notice.

It would be like dating someone and discovering they've cheated on you. They may truly be sorry and never do it again, but it's always in the back of your mind, renting space. Whether it's dating or supervising, you shouldn't let things slide. You've got to eliminate things that rent space in your head, so that you can use that space for helpful and productive thoughts.

If employees start developing a track record of dropping the ball and renting too much space in my head, then there is a problem. If the problem persists, there's an eviction notice.

If you know someone who micromanages people, this concept of employees renting space in your head doesn't apply. That's because micromanagers are in the habit of letting staff rent space in their head and following up behind them. It's no wonder micromanagers are usually quite busy but contribute very little to the bottom line. They usually try to hire people who need to be micromanaged because such employees fit their mold. In the beginning, many employees may need some degree of hand-holding, but after a while a good manager should step progressively further back and let employees do their job. Micromanaging also alienates good employees, and eventually they will seek employment where they can do a job and be appreciated for their accomplishments. People need to have space to be creative *and even make mistakes.*

The bottom line is that you have beliefs that produce reactions and results. Be they negative or positive, some of your beliefs are good tenants and worth keeping, while others are worthless and can't be evicted fast enough. Later in the book, we'll talk more about the eviction process and where to find new tenants. For now, you should try to establish a solid prequalifying process for new candidates. Whenever you have an experience that has an emotional impact on you, decide if the lesson you think you've learned and the ensuing belief is helpful for your future. You can rent space in your head, but don't let the first applicant have the place. Prequalify, and only let the really good ones in.

SUMMARY

■ We react to things because of our culture, parents, grandparents, schooling, teachers, religion, and genetics.

■ It will help if you consider *why* you react in certain ways.

▌ Childhood experiences can influence you for a lifetime.

▌ You can use your intellect to overcome and reprogram your "natural reactions."

▌ Recognizing and analyzing your beliefs is the first step toward being able to control and manage them in your own best interest.

Chapter 4

You Can't Change What You Don't Acknowledge

I can remember times when something strange went wrong with my car and then the problem cleared up by itself. Then it came back, and it went away again. It seems as though car problems frequently go away just as you're pulling up to the service department. The annoying thing is that now you have to hope your car will start having the mechanical problem again while it's in for service so the mechanic can see the problem and fix it. What's even more irritating is that you're going to get charged by the mechanic, even if he doesn't find the real problem. Unfortunately you can't get mad at him because he can't be expected to fix a problem that doesn't appear to be there in the first place.

It's really nothing more complicated than, you can't fix what doesn't appear to be broken. Or, put another way, *you can't change what you don't acknowledge.*

Have you ever tried to talk to friends about a personality flaw that they have, which everyone else sees except them? It's hard even to bring up things like that because you don't want to hurt their feelings. But the real problem is that if they don't recognize the problem to begin with, you usually have to be so forceful that you're in danger of jeopardizing that friendship. If their denial is especially strong, they'll just think you're nuts, or hypersensitive, or just plain mean.

This same mentality applies to departments, sales teams, divisions, companies, and even entire industries. I'm sure that if you thought about it for just a few minutes, you could come up with a few people in your company who just don't get it, but if they did, it could change their world.

A friend of mine related an experience like this, which happened recently with a leading software company. As part of an independent training company, he was teaching a three-hour seminar on how to use a particular program. There were approximately 500 people in the audience, and one of the management folks from the software company was invited to attend. After watching most of the session, she complained that the training was well over the heads of the audience and that the training was too expert and didn't appear to be directed at the proper target market.

---

*I'm sure that if you thought about it for just a few minutes,
you could come up with a few people who just don't get it,
but if they did, it could change their world.*

Ironically, every single feedback form from the attendees that day was overwhelmingly positive about the training. Not one single attendee said the material was over his or her head or that the trainer was hard to understand. My friend invited the manager from the software company to look over the feedback forms as soon as they were collected from exiting patrons so she could see that he wasn't just showing her selected responses. She was open-mouthed, amazed. She simply couldn't believe that every attendee was thrilled. She was astonished that some independent training company understood the end user so much better than a professional from the company that actually makes the software.

The back story on this particular situation is that the software company wasn't convinced that an independent trainer could present their program as well as the manufacturer could. The training company could have bragged about their abilities all day long and have never convinced the software maker of their skills. Even when the software company sent an actual representative to review the training in person, she still wasn't convinced. Only after seeing the unfiltered responses from attendees was she finally convinced. The relatively small software training company got a contract with a major software maker because of the real-world evidence.

> **POWER TIP**
>
> You can't change what you don't acknowledge.

Until then, the software maker wasn't willing to acknowledge that an outside training company could possibly present their product better than the manufacturer could. They only changed their opinion when, in the face of overwhelming evidence, they were forced to acknowledge it.

The saddest thing I often see is people who attend seminars or read books that offer solid, helpful, insightful information, but these people don't go far enough with their beliefs. They may agree with everything. They think, "yep, that's good stuff! I agree with that for sure. . . ." But their life is in total disarray. Their professional life reflects the gap between agreement and action as well.

Agreeing to all this great stuff on an intellectual level is one thing, *believing* it is another. To me, believing means that you move from *intellectualizing* something to *internalizing* it. Some people don't want to believe because *belief requires action*, and action usually takes people out of their comfort zone. Some people put off acknowledging because they would have to make a change, and people are uncomfortable with change. Another problem is that in order to acknowledge and change you have to admit that what you're doing isn't working. Admitting that they are wrong is simply beyond some people.

Regardless of the reason that people don't want to recognize their problems, the issue comes down to the simple concept of denial. People in denial don't want to acknowledge problems because doing so might be too painful.

Whether consciously or subconsciously, not everyone prefers to be in denial. Some people find it more painful *not* to change. For some people, myself included, *not* acknowledging and *not* growing are more painful than denial.

Whenever the results you're getting aren't consistent with your goals, the next logical step should be to look for ways to change, or at least look for ways in which you can be more open to change. Even though denial may seem to be a benefit, in that you avoid problems in the short term, denial and procrastination simply don't provide consistent, positive outcomes in the long run. What's more, procrastination leads to an unfulfilling lifestyle. If you want to live a rich, full life, you've got to commit to eliminating procrastination as much as possible.

Whenever the results you're getting aren't consistent with your goals, the next logical step should be to look for ways to change.

It's important that you understand this chapter's emphasis within the framework of the book's overall structure. As you begin to embrace the foundational principle—"you cannot change what you don't acknowledge"—you should keep in mind that this is only Chapter 4. *Don't be disappointed or discard this concept as unusable because it doesn't work for you right away.* In fact, you shouldn't expect to make the big, powerful changes in your life using this concept alone. The reason is that you can't change what you don't acknowledge isn't even a tool. It's a foundational principle.

Because we aren't yet discussing tools and techniques for taking life-changing steps, it will be best to simply read and absorb the material in this chapter and wait until later to seek ways to apply it.

You shouldn't expect to make the big, powerful changes in your life using this concept alone.

Every day, I see people wearing blinders in both their business and personal lives. As a business owner and entrepreneur, one of the necessary evils in my business is that I have to let people go from my organization, in most cases because they just won't see what they need to change, even when I give them all the answers.

For example, occasionally we'll have people in our office who are new to sales, and their numbers are lower than they should be. I'll sit down with them and try to help them out. My staff knows I've been in sales for many years, and they recognize that I know my company's products and services better than anyone. In a heart-to-heart, I'll tell them that their numbers are down because they aren't making enough calls. Sometimes, the response I get is, "Oh, I'm making calls. I'm on the phone all day long!"

Now, there are people on my team who respond in open-minded ways; they are still with me. If they ask me how to wrap up sales calls more quickly, so they can place a greater number of calls, I know they get it. If they come to me when they see their numbers are down and ask for help or coaching, I know they get it. My experience is that people who are willing to learn and aren't defensive will grow and become exceptional team members.

People who are defensive, or argue about their numbers, don't necessarily question my experience, product knowledge, or sales ability. They just don't believe that they did anything wrong. They even think that *I* must be wrong about how many calls they're making. Sure, sales are down, but it must be because of something else.

In order for someone to be able to recognize problems and make changes, several thought processes must be in place. They must have an open mind, a humble attitude, and the ability to not take themselves too seriously. This may be hard or even impossible, depending on where they are in their life, but they need to be honest with themselves.

So let's go back to my original observation. I said, "You're not making enough calls." In this scenario, what must change is that they must make more calls. No excuses, just more calls. No emotion, no extra time in the office, just more calls. Because you can't change what you don't acknowledge, if they continue to insist that they are already making enough calls, it won't be long before they're on their way out the door.

Excuses are pointless and just a waste of time. They don't help you overcome challenges, and they don't help you realize what you need to change. Although there are all kinds of things in life that help us avoid personal responsibility, this doesn't mean we should. We've got to quit blaming other people and other things for our failures in life. We live in an irresponsible world, where many people blame anyone and everyone else for their failures, but these same people don't hesitate to take the credit for successes.

Let's say that you and I are close friends, and I tell you, "I've had it. I'm throwing in the towel." Whose fault is it that I'm quitting? That's easy, it's mine. A good friend wouldn't pull any punches, and you'd tell it like it is. It's my choice, my fault if I quit.

But consider this, my father was murdered, and I miss him. *Now* whose fault is it that I want to throw in the towel or constantly make excuses for my failures? Truthfully, it's still my fault.

Okay . . . but I lost all my savings paying for my newborn's special needs, and hospital bills ate me alive. *Now* whose fault is it that I'm quitting? Give me a break. My wife said my son isn't even mine! My uncle was killed in a plane crash. How much can one person be expected to take? It's just not fair! I think I have every right to quit or at least make a bunch of excuses for failing!

But if I do quit now, if I throw in the towel after all that, whose fault is it *really*? It's still mine. For some reason, our society wants to enable people who make excuses because something in life isn't fair, but the bottom line is that quitting is *my* fault.

So if *you* want to quit, if you've got a ton of great reasons to quit, *whose fault is it really if you quit?*

Are you limiting your potential because you are blaming others or even yourself?

People are suing restaurants because they claim it's the restaurant's fault that they are fat. Give me a break! As a society, we need to take a collective breath and say to ourselves, "I am responsible for my own actions and the results of my actions." The craziness doesn't seem to stop. It is in every part of our society. I recently attended helicopter training school and heard about a similar circumstance.

As a society, we need to take a collective breath and say to ourselves, "I am responsible for my own actions and the results of my actions."

Whenever you land a helicopter, you are supposed to idle for a few minutes to let the engine cool down. Then, after you shut the engine off, it's standard practice to let the rotors come to a complete stop before exiting the craft. Sure, there are times when people exit or board helicopters while the rotors are spinning, and there are times when people ride in cars without seat belts. If you can avoid being careless, you should. It's just common sense. What's more, because of the way they are built, certain types of helicopters have rotors that are more exposed and potentially closer to pedestrians.

In one particular circumstance, after landing, the pilot walked immediately to the back of his helicopter without following each of the standard post-landing procedures. As a result of the spinning tail rotor, he lost his arm. Keep in mind, this was the pilot! Did he know that his helicopter has a tail rotor? Of course! Did he know the blades keep spinning after the engine stops? Sure. Did he do something stupid? You bet. Can you dream of a way he could try to blame his mistake on someone else? He sued the helicopter manufacturer. The basis for his suit was that the Danger sign by the tail rotor wasn't big enough. If he didn't follow standard procedure, do you think he's going to read a sign of any size? Do you think this guy would still have his arm if the entire side of the helicopter had the letters "D-A-N-G-E-R" in bold, red type? Based on this guy's personal irresponsibility, nothing would have saved his arm unless the manufacturer built the helicopter with a seat beside the tail rotor, manned by a company official with a bullhorn whose job it was to scream and remind you that the tail rotor can blend you into pieces. There was no defect in the helicopter. Besides, common sense safety procedures are the responsibility of the pilot!

Thank goodness the judge saw right through this, and the pilot lost the case. This shouldn't have even gone to court, but this kind of thing happens when people don't acknowledge certain truths about themselves.

POWER TIP

Set your goals based on logic, not emotions.

As you consider the principle—you can't change what you don't acknowledge—it's important to realize that change won't happen from simply acknowledging a problem. Neither acknowledgment or even belief is a magic bullet that makes positive change happen automatically. In fact, there are varying degrees of belief and even different kinds of beliefs about any given problem or solution. In the following example, remember that the how of believing will be answered in Chapter 10 and Chapter 14, so don't push to understand the how just yet.

Consider people who smoke. It's possible that they may not even think about the possibility that anything bad will come of their habit and there is absolutely no reason to even consider quitting. Later, they might start to acknowledge that smoking is generally bad, and they might even acknowledge that someday it will affect them too. At this point, our smokers are in the acknowledgment stage.

Neither acknowledgment or even belief is a magic bullet that makes positive change happen automatically.

When our smokers start adding up the financial and interpersonal costs of smoking, and they start to see negative health effects from years of breathing tar smoke, our smokers may begin to believe that smoking is bad. They may even believe that they should quit smoking. So now they have a belief. Does that mean they will quit? Do you know people who still smoke in spite of their apparent belief that they should quit?

A smoker will only quit when the belief changes from, "I should quit or "I must quit" or "I'll try to quit," to the much more effective belief, "I will quit." In the words of Yoda the Jedi Master, "There is no 'try.' Either *do* or *do not*." Once the smoker believes he *will* quit, his actions will be consistent with that belief, and he *will* quit.

Now of course there are extenuating circumstances in this example. Some people may change beliefs midway and begin to smoke again. Their belief that they are too weak to stay away from cigarettes may be stronger than their belief that they have to quit. Another element is that new, empowering beliefs are only possible when the believer has control over the necessary circumstances. For example, a belief that you'll win the lottery will not necessarily make it happen. That's irrational optimism!

A smoker will only quit when the belief changes from, "I should quit or "I must quit" or "I'll try to quit," to the much more effective belief, "I will quit."

In later chapters we'll discuss the tools for discovering the things that are holding you back, help you identify some of the best steps you can take to eliminate limiting beliefs and behaviors, help you decide if a belief is an empowering and appropriate belief, and help you master these new beliefs, which will yield the best possible results in any circumstance.

For now, simply take a couple of minutes and write down on paper some of the negative results you're getting in your personal and professional life. Focus first on the poor results. What would you like to change? Is there something you've hoped or wished would get better but just didn't seem to improve in spite of your efforts?

Consider the possibility that you may have been ignoring some aspect of the negative situation because it would mean that you have been wrong.

Here comes the hard part. Consider the possibility that you may have been ignoring some aspect of the negative situation because it would mean that you have been wrong. Take a deep breath, and try to put yourself in a humble frame of mind. Then, on the same pad of paper below the negative results you've written down, write this phrase, "Because improving results is more important than my pride, I'm willing to admit I may have been wrong about my approach to these problems. Something I haven't considered before is. . . ." Then make a list of new ideas.

Something I haven't considered before is. . . .

You're not looking for things you've tried that didn't work. You need to discover those things you may have considered but didn't try or *new* things that you haven't acknowledged at all. Finally, keep these items handy as you read the rest of the book, so you can use them as a starting point for making improvements in your career and personal life.

I hope this excites and inspires you to keep reading, but make sure you don't just jump straight to Chapters 12–15 right now. I want to share with you some more foundational information first. Most people need to unlearn some things they think they know before the tools in Chapters 12–15 can have maximum impact.

Right now I believe it's time for you to turn the page so that you can unlearn a few pop-psychology lies, and then those chapters will really *energize* your life and your thinking!

SUMMARY

- Sometimes you can be too close to a problem to see it.

- It takes more than just a casual effort to recognize your own challenges.

- Once you recognize your problems in business and life, you have to commit to change them if you ever want things to improve.

■ Even though denial may offer the appearance of a benefit, in that you avoid problems in the short term, denial and procrastination simply don't provide consistent, positive outcomes in the long run.

■ At this stage you should try to uncover the things which you have denied in the past. Simple recognition doesn't automatically result in change. You'll learn how to change things later in the book.

■ Excuses are pointless and just a waste of time. They don't help you overcome challenges and they don't help you realize what you need to change.

■ Regardless of how bad your life seems or how "unfair" things have been in your life, it's still your own responsibility, and no one else's, to make changes.

Chapter 5

WHEN LIFE GIVES YOU LEMONS, DON'T DRINK THE LEMONADE

A friend of mine used to say, "When life gives you lemons, make lemonade!" It almost didn't matter what the circumstance, she always said it. Initially, there may appear to be truth in this advice. It sounds logical and optimistic. In the real world, though, when life (or your business) gives you lemons *don't drink the lemonade . . .* at least not right away.

When something big and bad happens in your life, it's rare that you can simply look at the bright side and move on (at least not right away). If you're not ready to move on for one reason or another, trying to force yourself to move on too soon can cause more damage, depression, and feelings of failure. Essentially, the issue is timing or, to be more accurate, *personal* timing. Personal timing is based on things like your experience and past challenges, intellectual knowledge, your personality, and your style.

Whether someone else tells you or you tell yourself to move on or just get over it, you can only move on if you have the right attitude. Haven't you had someone give you the just-get-over-it speech, which just made you much more upset? You probably thought, *You don't understand. I just can't move on.* Then just a day or two later, you have a conversation with someone who just tells you to get over it. You shake your head and say, "You're right. I really have to get over it. It's time to move on."

Another thing that determines the timing for you to drink the lemonade is the size of the lemon. The bigger the lemon, the worse the problem, and the more time you may need to get over the pain before you can make lemonade out of your lemons.

The good news is that timing is proportional, not absolute. For one person, it might normally take a month to get over a divorce, and for someone else it might normally take a year or more. (In fact, some people never get over their problems.) The better news is that you can use things like intellectual knowledge and the tools from this book to speed up your normal time frame. Maybe you need to go through 50 steps to be in a place where you're ready to overcome a lemon and move on. In later chapters, you'll discover tools that can help you do things like modify beliefs and behaviors, and you'll discover that there are ways to speed up your personal timing. Using the right tools, you can accomplish your 50 steps in days rather than months.

The bigger the lemon, the worse the problem, and the more time you may need to get over the pain before you can make lemonade out of your lemons.

Don't fall into the trap of using personal timing as an excuse for inaction. I've just given you a factual principle with a great deal of power. The principle is that you may not be ready to move on right away. If you use that principle as an excuse to avoid any action, you're lying to yourself, and you are in danger of never moving on. If you use the principle to understand intellectually that you may not be ready to move on, but there are things you can do to help you get ready to move, then you've unleashed the power of the concept, and it becomes an empowering principle instead of an excuse.

You know where I've been in life, so you know that my advice comes from the school of hard knocks. More than once, something painful has happened in my life that I was determined to get over. I've used this method several times in various forms, and it works well for me when big, painful things have happened. Because I don't want you to think that this works on only one particular type of problem, I'll leave the topic out of this explanation. I just want you to focus on my method and consider whether something like this might help you get past some major problem in life or business.

Using the right tools, you can accomplish your 50 steps in days rather than months.

I started by telling myself to move on. For some reason, the mantra "just move on" didn't work. Once I *realized* I couldn't move on because I wasn't ready, I thought about what would need to happen for me to be ready. I pictured a time in the future when I was over my problem, and I reasoned that I would need to experience the negative thoughts about my problem again and again until thinking about my lemon was just a non-emotional part of my past, rather than an emotional, painfully debilitating thought. I decided to relive my lemon again and again. I concentrated on the bad stuff. I thought about it constantly. I experienced as much pain as I could fit into each day—until I was numb. Finally, I had experienced the pain of my problem so much that I could begin to move on.

Now I don't recommend this approach for everyone, and it doesn't work for every situation, but what does work is to do whatever you can to take as many steps as possible to move past your lemon.

If you're trying to help someone else get past a divorce or business loss or some major life challenge, you must be empathetic first. Be sure your friend is ready before you push him to move on. Many times, people don't know how to help a grieving friend, so they just tell their friend to get over it. Maybe they're just trying to help, but trying to force someone to move on too early is such a bad thing to do that it would be better to say nothing. It's better to have a heart without words, than words without a heart.

Trying to force someone to move on too early is such a bad thing to do that it would be better to say nothing.

I recall spending time with a close friend who had been recently widowed, and she shared with me that many of her friends kept telling her to move on. Move on!? She'd been married for over 30 years, and her husband had only died a few months earlier. I told her to keep crying her eyes out. When people told her she should move on, she felt even weaker as a person. She thought that she should be able to follow the advice of her friends. She felt more than just weak; she felt that something must be wrong with her because she couldn't move on. Her friends meant well, but their comments actually made her feel worse.

Over 30 years of marriage, and only 3 months to cry? Give me a break. It's not time for her to drink the lemonade. She had a huge lemon to deal with. When it comes down to being ready to move on, this is what you must realize: *Time doesn't heal all wounds. You do.*

When you're helping friends, make sure you give them time to absorb their circumstances before you push them to ignore their emotional attachment to the past and simply live happily ever after. Having said that, there will come a time for intervention. If you're close with the friend you're trying to help, you'll need to use your good judgment to distinguish between the time she needs to experience necessary pain, and the possibility that her depressed mood is becoming a habit that needs to be broken. Some people need a close personal friend or a good professional counselor to help them take the first steps toward moving on.

When you're helping friends, make sure you give them time to absorb their circumstances before you push them to ignore their emotional attachment to the past and simply live happily ever after.

I have a friend who survived more than one rape. Just one assault like this is incredibly difficult for almost anyone to deal with, but she had lived through three! Now, this may not seem logical if you don't know someone who has been attacked, but often victims blame themselves for being attacked. Imagine having been attacked on more than one occasion by different people. In a circumstance like that, it's almost inevitable that the victim would blame herself. She did.

Because of my friendship with her and my background in human behavior, I knew it was time for her to get out. She had been alone with her thoughts long enough, and she needed to be made to get away from her house for a while. My second wife and I stopped by her house and made her go out with us. We took her to another friend's house for an informal gathering and got her mind off her troubles. This was a case of forcing someone to drink the lemonade.

It wouldn't have worked if we waited for her to tell us she was ready. My wife and I knew it was time, and we intervened. *You need to be really careful here* because not everyone can make this kind of decision for friends. If you do it wrong you can ruin your friendship or hurt the person you're trying to help, or both.

Really big things can come from moving beyond life's problems. You know *my* story but let me tell you about a woman who has a tremendous following and runs a multimillion-dollar enterprise. She is a true success story.

Carol Gardener has been featured on *Oprah* and has a greeting card, book, and poster business that earns millions. It's based on her wit and wisdom coupled with great photos of her English bulldog Zelda, in humorous costumes. Beginning with a winning entry in a greeting card contest, Gardener continued her greeting card success by creating an entire line of greeting cards. Zelda is now featured on cards, posters, figurines, snow globes, journals, notebooks, in four published books, and even on a line of Zelda apparel. What many Zelda fans don't know is that Zelda wasn't some corporate marketing department's brainchild. Zelda was a dog that was purchased because of Gardener's difficult divorce. She wanted to move on, but she wasn't sure how. Her lemons were the divorce, and her lemonade was a funny-looking English bulldog.

Following the suggestion of a friend, she jokes that she had two options: get a therapist or get a dog. She got a dog and the rest is history.

SUMMARY

- When something overwhelming and negative happens in your business or life, it's rare that you can simply look at the bright side and move on immediately.

- You can use things like intellectual knowledge and the tools from this book to speed up your normal healing time.

- Often you can't move on until you're ready, but you can change how long it takes to be ready.

Chapter 6

IRRATIONAL OPTIMISM

O ne of the things I wish for you as you read this book is that you'll come away from the experience with an enhanced ability to make very fine distinctions about emotions and perceptions. This book is filled with explanations and examples, which I hope will help you understand nuances that might appear to be splitting hairs, but in the long run are quite different. For example, one of this book's chapters is called "The Hoax of Positive Thinking," while another is called "Positive Thinking Is a Lie, But It's a Start." Until you actually delve into the content of these two chapters, their titles seem to suggest two totally opposite views.

If you take *any* topic (cars, wine, cell phones, cooking), there will be those who know the details of the topic far better than the general public. True aficionados can recognize practically imperceptible differences in the grade of a seasoning used in a recipe. True experts can often tell by taste, where and when a wine originated. In each case, the differences may be subtle but with expert training and practice, almost anyone can be taught to recognize these distinctions. It's important that you try to study the explanations and examples I've provided, so you can actually begin to make distinctions yourself. And with practice, the distinctions become easier to identify.

To draw the analogy even further, if you were looking for an expert to restore your vintage automobile, you'd likely prefer to hire someone who had worked on restoring similar cars before and you'd probably feel that you had hit the jackpot if you could find a mechanic who owned the exact same vehicle you intend to restore. If you planned to do your own work on your vehicle, taking lessons and advice from someone who had been there himself is what most people would prefer. So when it comes to personal growth, business attitudes, tools for overcoming challenges, and moving to the next level both personally and professionally, I will occasionally seem to be focusing on making distinctions that initially appear trivial. Each time you can grasp one of those subtle distinctions, you'll have mastered another tool on your way to your own success. You need to be in the right frame of mind (alert and willing to learn) and then truly study the concepts in this chapter for them to make sense and not sound like double-talk.

> *It's important that you try to study the explanations and examples I've provided, so you can actually begin to make distinctions yourself.*

In fact, simply understanding that the distinctions exist puts you in a class above the average citizen. For example, most people would consider the terms "optimism" and "positive thinking" to be synonyms representing a way of thinking. Some pop psychologists would go even further and say that positive thinking and optimism are a complete solution to bad life experiences and are a method to overcome challenges or even tragedies. That kind of oversimplification does more harm than good. It keeps people from understanding the truth about all of the various types of optimism and positive thinking and how you can use them as an ingredient, in combination with many other ingredients, which is part of a recipe for achieving your goals.

If you hear an expert say that optimism is the key to achieving your goals or fixing your problems or living your dreams, you need to immediately realize that the expert is oversimplifying to the point of absurdity. That's like saying, "Water is the key to losing weight." Are we talking about swimming? Does that mean we should eliminate food? Does that mean to drink more? Or less? Or maybe it means that we should hose down our lunch before eating. You see, it's crazy to over simplify that much! I can't tell you how many experts offer that kind of shallow advice when it comes to personal and professional self-improvement, but now that you know what to watch for, you won't be fooled by their simple answers anymore.

> *If you hear an expert say that optimism is the key to achieving your goals or fixing your problems or living your dreams, you need to immediately realize that the expert is oversimplifying to the point of absurdity.*

Irrational optimism is one of those subtle distinctions that appears to be hard to understand at first, but once you understand it, you'll be able to use it to your benefit.

You can spot irrational optimism when people's actions are based on unbalanced or ridiculous ideas of success or positive outcomes. Let me share with you an example of how easy it can be to become irrationally optimistic.

Think back to the first time you went bowling. You slipped on a pair of those funny-looking alley shoes and spent all kinds of time finding just the right ball to fit your hand. In spite of your preparation, you know practically nothing about the game itself, especially how to keep score. If you're like most people, you know that a strike is great, a spare is good, and a gutter ball is terrible.

You can spot irrational optimism when people's actions are based on unbalanced or ridiculous ideas of success or positive outcomes.

It's your turn, and you walk up to pick up your ball. You fit your fingers snugly into the holes, and you step up onto the wooden floor. You hold the ball under your chin with both hands (because that's what you've seen everyone else doing), and you make your move. You take a few long strides, and as you approach the fowl line, you let go of the ball . . . and bam! It slams hard onto the lane and rolls into the gutter. A gutter ball. It's probably what you expected.

You wait your turn and try it again. As you keep bowling, you get a little better. You throw the ball again, and now you knock down four pins. Next time up, against all odds you roll a strike! You're thrilled, and your friends are clapping and cheering for you.

It's almost your turn again, and you start thinking about your strike. Here you are, never bowled a day in your life, and all of a sudden you get a strike! A crazy thing happens at this point. Because you've made your first strike, you *truly believe* that you can do it again on your next turn.

So you grab that ball with confidence and step up onto the lane. Pacing yourself, you stride confidently forward and throw the ball. Your confidence is high, your approach and release feel good, and as the ball rolls down the alley you see it veer off to one side and into the gutter. Another gutter ball.

You may very well end up leaving your first day without ever getting another strike. Fooling yourself into believing that you could get a second strike, immediately after your first one, was irrationally optimistic.

It's easy to be irrationally optimistic when you don't understand all of the factors that go into throwing strikes consistently. You don't have the experience. It is far more likely that your first strike was the result of a few accidental factors coming together than the skills you acquired during the first two frames.

But because most people believe in their own abilities, frequently beyond logic and reason, it's easy to become irrationally optimistic. Often, this comes when you receive some type of positive influence or feedback, like the bowling strike, or a friend who thinks it helps to tell you that your idea is really great when it's not. Optimism itself isn't even the problem; the problem is that irrational optimism gives us false hope. If you're talking about the first time you went bowling, false hope is no big deal. (There are times when false hope can be a useful tool, but we'll talk about that later.) If you're talking about business plans, financial goals, personal goals, or relationship expectations, irrational optimism can be a really bad thing.

The problem is that irrational optimism gives us false hope.

A great example of irrational optimism is the TV show *American Idol*. People from all over the country audition and then a few, select finalists compete to sign a multimillion dollar recording contract. Literally, tens of thousands of people audition, but only one will walk away as the *American Idol*.

The judges that conduct the regional auditions usually ask each contestant two questions. The first is "Why do you want to be the next *American Idol*?" And the second is "Are *you* the next *American Idol*?" They all answer "yes" to the second question! Part of the fun audiences have watching the early phases of *American Idol* is the performances by people who are irrationally optimistic. It's hard to imagine that some of these competitors believe they have a shot when they obviously have no talent.

Everyone wants to be an American Idol. *Most don't come anywhere near qualifying, yet they're somehow under the impression that their talent is good enough to make a living at it.*

I have a saying in my office, *everyone wants to be an American Idol.* I use this saying when it comes to hiring people to join our sales team. We have a team of trainers that travel throughout the country and represent me at smaller events (we call these workshops) of 100 or fewer people. To qualify for this position, candidates must be great public speakers. We'll view some of the videos from those who think they qualify. We send them a one-page sample script. To qualify for an interview, they must send us a video of themselves presenting the sample script. Some of the audition tapes are horrific. *Everyone wants to be an American Idol.* Most don't come anywhere near qualifying, yet they're somehow under the impression that their speaking talent is good enough to make a living at it.

This kind of irrational optimism can cause us to make very foolish decisions and set ourselves up for serious failure. I've found that most people become very unrealistic when projecting their success, especially when setting a goal in an area where they may not have much experience. We seem to have a mental battle that goes on just beyond our conscious awareness. It takes place when we're planning what we'll be able to attain and when we think we can accomplish it. Here's what that internal conversation might sound like.

"I want to stay excited about my goal, so I'll tell myself that

I am going to hit this mark. I need to believe in this goal, however unreasonable it may be, because thinking about failing at my dream is far too painful. Because I don't want think about that failure, I'll just ignore being reasonable, I'll ignore planning for possible failure, and I'll just stay excited with the false hope of my dream."

The unfortunate shame of our unrealistic belief in our dreams is that when we avoid even considering a "Plan B," we are destined for deep disappointment or even depression when our goal doesn't come to fruition.

I've been just as guilty as anyone when it comes to being caught up in this kind of irrational optimism. I especially fell victim to all of this when I started getting more into personal growth and investigating some of this positive thinking stuff. I got the impression that all I would have to do is set a goal, pick a completion date, and voilà it was going to happen. Though that's an exaggeration of the process I became so discouraged because I usually missed my target altogether and if I did accomplish a goal it was never on time. Over time I realized I was a victim of irrational optimism.

The unfortunate shame of our unrealistic belief in our dreams is that when we avoid even considering a "Plan B," we are destined for deep disappointment or even depression when our goal doesn't come to fruition.

One important thing I came away with was the fact I realized that attaining our goals usually takes longer than we expect it to take. Once I realized this, I was able to take a more realistic approach to setting my goals. Previously I was setting my goals based on emotions, not logic, which set me up for a big fall.

In Chapter 10, "Be Prepared to Abort or Lose An Engine," you'll see that there is a place for negative thoughts like thinking about what to do if you don't reach a goal. Having a

"Plan-B" and being prepared for failure is one of the keys to avoiding irrational optimism.

A secondary problem that comes from irrational optimism is that people frequently create negative associations to setting our goals. When you set a goal with lots of emotion and an irrational amount of optimism and you don't achieve that goal, especially if that happens more than once, people can easily begin to think that setting goals is really a waste of time. We may reason, "Why set another goal? I'm just going to be disappointed when I don't reach it. Look at my last few goals. That was painful! I'll just avoid the pain by avoiding setting goals."

Maybe you've heard the trite sound bite that *"a goal is just a dream with a deadline."* That's ridiculous! That kind of over-simplification leaves out so many aspects of reality that it's destined to cause more harm than good for practically everyone. The only place this philosophy ever worked was in Disney movies from the '50s.

Maybe you've heard the trite sound bite that **"a goal is just a dream with a deadline."** *That's ridiculous!*

It may sound pessimistic at first but there is a much healthier way to look at your goals. The mindset that I now have toward attaining my goals is that it's never as easy as it seems and it's probably going to take longer that I think it will. I usually have to invest more blood, sweat, and tears than I originally planned. But my goal is worthwhile and I'm committed to making it happen in spite of the unseen challenges.

This is the beginning of a healthy attitude toward setting goals. Your goals can still be big and evoke powerful emotions but logic and planning must be a part of the mix. Your goals might even seem wildly optimistic or even impossible to others, but if you have a solid plan to achieve your goals and alternate plans of action for unexpected surprises along the way, your goals won't be irrationally optimistic.

Exactly how to plan for the roadblocks, delays, and unexpected circumstances will become clear in later chapters. For now though, if you understand that a dream or a wish isn't automatically a goal, then you're headed in the right direction.

You also need to make sure you don't get hung up on the timeline or investment not hitting your initial projections. Plan for mistakes and allow for a cushion in both financial and workforce commitments. How many times do you hear people on the news telling you how much a project is expected to cost and at the end of the project it ends up taking longer than expected and costing millions (or in the case of many government projects, billions) more?

Eventually you must come to the same realization I did. If you don't attain your goals on time it's not the end of the world. It's okay. Success should truly be a journey, not a destination.

A great way to get a handle on this and save yourself from being overly discouraged when you don't reach a goal on time or if your goal doesn't reach the level you'd like, is to realize that there is a cost to every goal. And you have to realize this before you start on your goal.

If you don't attain your goals on time it's not the end of the world.

If you ask almost anyone if they're willing to pay the price to reach their goal they answer yes. Then if you ask them, "What is the price that you'll have to pay to reach your goals?" most haven't taken the time to even figure that out! That's because it's easy to set a goal or have a dream if there's no investment associated with it. Once you tie a price to a dream and develop a plan of action, you've started to turn your dream into a goal and you've also exponentially increased the likelihood of achieving that goal.

It's true that facing the potential cost of our goal means facing reality and it may just burst our bubble. I don't know about you, but I'd rather burst my bubble now than get so deep into a project that I can't get back out. This helps me see things very realistically and it also helps remove some of the false hope.

If people who are inexperienced in relationships would do a better job realizing this before they got married, they wouldn't be so let down when the honeymoon euphoria wears off. If he burps out loud on the date, he's going to burp a lot louder after you marry him, and that's just the half of it.

I see this happen to so many people who start a business or get into sales. Due to their inexperience they have many unrealistic goals. I've known people who really had what it takes, but because they approached their project with unrealistic expectations, they went bankrupt or quit. Many of these people then vow never to take on another risk because it could happen again. It's really sad. If they looked at things just a bit more realistically without becoming so irrationally optimistic they would still be making their dreams come true.

Again, it may seem pessimistic to plan for things to take longer than you expect or cost more than you plan, but while you're preparing for the unexpected occurrences along the path to your goal, you also have to plan for success. If you really have a great goal or business plan, you need to plan for big-time success. I've seen business become so successful that they start losing business because they hadn't planned for so much success. Some companies (divisions, sales teams, individuals, and so forth) aren't prepared for their success and they miss opportunities or crash and burn because they couldn't meet demand. Part of your plan is to be ready for success that's even bigger than your goal.

Keep in mind that the focus of the planning I've suggested so far has included just you and no outside opinions. I've mentioned that others might believe that your goals are unrealistic or irrational and even if you value your friend's advice, it's more important for *you* to believe in your goals and to develop a complete plan for achieving them. And you need to fully develop your plan of action *before* you seek outside opinions. Then when you finally do seek outside opinions, consider what strengths of judgment and experience with that topic the other person has, if any. I'd be willing to bet that most of the *American Idol* contestants' mothers believe that their child is brilliantly gifted and a sure thing.

I've known people who really had what it takes, but because they approached their project with unrealistic expectations, they went bankrupt or quit.

In fact, parents and friends are often where we learn some of our irrational optimism. Parents don't do their kids any favors by telling them how wonderful they are, when they still need lots of practice at something. Of course there are times to comfort children and bolster their confidence, but in the long run it doesn't help a kid to continuously hear false praise.

Mentors are a good place to go when flushing out your plans because, presumably, they've been there before. There are pros and cons about using mentors. On the plus side they have experience and think in ways that your other friends might not. On the negative side, your plans might be so innovative or outside your mentor's expertise that they can't visualize your project any better than the average person.

Consider looking for a pessimist. What I mean is, don't seek just positive feedback to supercharge your enthusiasm and ego, look for negative feedback too. Use the "problems" that friends and mentors express to further improve your plan, marketing message, timeline, budget, or other aspects of your plan. Once you do all this research and planning, if you're still the only one that thinks your idea is possible, it's not necessarily time to give in. You might just see something no one else can see. Just make sure you're really listening to and planning for the inevitable negative circumstances along the way and when road blocks appear, don't ignore them optimistically. That's irrational. Develop a plan to overcome the road block or find another path around it.

Mentors are a good place to go when flushing out your plans because, presumably, they've been there before. There are pros and cons about using mentors.

Now here's a real twist for you. There are times that being irrationally optimistic can work in your favor. I would consider it relatively rare but it does happen. It's kind of explained by the expression, "you don't know what you don't know."

Some have succeeded because they didn't know what they were getting into. They went into a project a bit blind, and in spite of the steep learning curve and their thoughts of quitting, they chose to learn from the experience and keep pursuing their goal.

I regularly look back to some of the things that I did when I first got into business and it makes me laugh (now). Though I was incredibly irrationally optimistic, I at least moved forward. I fell flat on my face but learned from that. I bounced back up and fell again and again and again. My irrational optimism rarely delivered my goal but it usually moved me toward something positive. Something I wanted.

Once I learned to eliminate (or at least minimize) irrational optimism I have been able to reach goals more quickly and with far fewer surprises. Because success feeds success, achieving business and life goals keeps encouraging me to set and achieve more and bigger goals.

Once I learned to eliminate (or at least minimize) irrational optimism I have been able to reach goals more quickly and with far fewer surprises.

Learning this on my own was a hard lesson but here's what I've found: Be as logical and realistic as you can by thinking about a step-by-step plan for each of your business and life goals and the costs involved. And remember if you don't attain one of your goals in the allotted time, it's okay. It's not the end of the world. Just don't quit and *don't let others rent space in your head!*

SUMMARY

▌ Some distinctions in this book may seem like splitting hairs, but once you understand the topics more completely, the differences will become much more apparent.

▌ There's a difference between optimism and irrational optimism and you can determine which is which.

▌ Attaining goals usually takes longer than you think.

▌ Having a Plan-B doesn't mean you expect or welcome failure of your primary plan, it's just good business. Always be ready to keep moving forward.

▌ The right attitude toward attaining goals is that it's never as easy as it seems and it's probably going to take longer that you think it will. You usually have to invest more blood, sweat, and tears than you originally planned. But your goal is worthwhile and you should be committed to making it happen in spite of the unseen challenges.

▌ If you don't attain your goals on time it's not the end of the world. It's okay. Just don't use that as an excuse to quit.

▌ Achieving a business or personal goal will cost something.

▌ A mentor and even a pessimist can be helpful when you're reviewing your goals or business plans because they'll help you see things which you had overlooked because of your optimism.

▌ Expect that your plans will change as you move toward your goals.

Chapter 7

THE HOAX OF POSITIVE THINKING

POSITIVE THINKING IS OVERRATED

One of the most common pieces of advice you'll hear from people is to "just think positive." Somehow, by just remembering happier times in your life, you're supposed to be able to use those good feelings to overcome your current negative life experiences. It sounds logical, and it gives people something to do so they are busy working on a project to start feeling better. The problem is that positive thinking is a lie, and it doesn't work!

THERE ARE FOUR KEY REASONS WHY POSITIVE THINKING DOESN'T WORK

First, positive thinking, even if it seems to work, doesn't last long. Second, positive thinking is absolutely ineffective if you're not at the right point in your life. Third, when it doesn't work, people think they're not doing it right, and they become more discouraged. Fourth, positive thinking is

Power Tip

Hope keeps
everything alive.

often presented as the solution rather than a simple, limited-use tool. There are other reasons that positive thinking doesn't work, and these will become apparent as this chapter unfolds.

Positive thinking is like spray paint on rust, it doesn't last long. This statement illustrates perfectly the first problem with positive thinking. If you master the positive thinking exercises, which experts tell you will help improve your situation, you may appear outwardly to have overcome your problem(s). Inwardly, however, you are not convinced that your problems have been resolved, and the continuing underlying issues must be resolved for you to overcome your problems.

Positive thinking is like spray paint on rust, it doesn't last long.

Ironically, some personalities can even develop further, deeper problems if they simply mask their symptoms by thinking positively. How many times have you heard TV interviews with family members or former schoolmates of some criminal or suicide victim who say, ". . . but he seemed like everything was fine"?

My spray paint analogy comes from the fact that I enjoy all aspects of aviation, including the mechanics and body work on planes and helicopters. If you spray paint a rusted spot, you can make it look better for a while, but the repair won't last long, and the underlying problem is still there because you're only masking the situation. The problems will always grow worse under the surface. For a spray-painted repair to last, you need to prepare the surface first. Sanding the surface, removing corrosion and grease, and priming the surface are all necessary to make paint last.

In the same way, you need to handle all of your problems directly first. This book is loaded with insights to help you understand what the problems are with pop-psychology solutions in and real-world tools to help you overcome your problems and get the results you want.

The second problem with positive thinking is that it's absolutely ineffective if you aren't in the right place in your life. For positive thinking to have the remotest possibility of helping, you must have the right mind-set first.

You wouldn't expect someone in the throes of grief after losing a spouse in a traffic accident to be able to snap out of it or look at the bright side. At least, not right away. When I lost my father and uncle, I heard a lot of this kind of drivel. In fact, I came to hate the following phrases: "Look on the bright side . . ." "It's not that bad . . ." "It will get better . . ." and the prize winner at the very bottom of my list—"It could be worse."

You wouldn't expect someone in the throes of grief after losing a spouse in a traffic accident to be able to snap out of it or look at the bright side. At least, not right away.

I guess people wanted to help me and make me feel better, and in retrospect it's nice to know that people cared, but telling me to feel better was the last thing that I needed. Positive thinking was worthless for me, because I wasn't ready.

Keep in mind that people don't mean any harm, and they're not stupid when they say these things. Most times, they truly have your best interests at heart, and they mean well. It's just that they aren't trained communicators or they don't understand that these platitudes don't really help.

Let me illustrate a step further what I mean by being ready. Imagine that I invite you over to my house, and we're going to bake some cookies. I get everything all mixed up, and we put the cookies in the oven. Mmm, they smell so good. I hand you a cookie, and as you take a bite, you look at me and say, "Gary, something doesn't taste right." We look over at the counter and discover that you're absolutely right. I forgot to put the eggs in the mix.

You don't have to be a professional chef here, but wouldn't you agree that for most cookies, not all, but for most cookies to taste right you usually have to have eggs in the ingredients? Sure!

So I go over to the counter and take the eggs, and I proceed to crack them and put them in the bowl. I get the raw eggs all mixed up. Now I take your cookie back from you and dip it in the raw eggs. (I wish I could see your face now.)

But, didn't we agree, not even 10 seconds ago, that we had to have eggs in the ingredients? And wouldn't you also agree that there is a difference between having eggs on the cookie or in the cookies? So you think about it; if we want these cookies to taste right, we are going to have to start—you guessed it—from scratch.

We had all of the right ingredients but the problem wasn't the eggs themselves; it's that they needed to go into the recipe in the right order. Positive thinking will never work if the right time for it hasn't come.

The third point is that when positive thinking doesn't work, lots of people think they're doing something wrong, and they become even more discouraged. I don't know about you, but for me, after reading some of the positive thinking books and listening to experts, I get the impression that they believe all we have to do is just say to ourselves, "life is great, it's gonna be a great day no matter what, and everything's gonna work out just fine!"

The third point is that when positive thinking doesn't work, lots of people think they're doing something wrong, and they become even more discouraged.

I think you'll agree that life is a bit more complicated than that.

As I said earlier, I have been in the depths of clinical depression (and I think I earned it). I wanted to find out how I could keep going, but "think positive" seemed to be the only answer people could offer. I assure you it was no help. I kept trying to think positive, but my mind was so full of negative thoughts, and I was in such a low place that positive thinking didn't do a thing for me.

The real problem was more than not being ready for positive thinking. My big problem was that so many people said positive thinking was the answer that I was sure the problem must be me. I must be doing something wrong. As if I didn't have enough problems, now I wasn't doing positive thinking correctly. I didn't need that kind of pressure.

My big problem was that so many people said positive thinking was the answer that I was sure the problem must be me. I must be doing something wrong.

Positive thinking can work, but only when two things are in place first. And you must master these two things in order for positive thinking to work for you. Without these two ingredients, you're dipping your cookies into the raw eggs. You must have the right timing and the right attitude.

Let's discuss timing. It truly is all about timing. If a man's wife has just told him that his baby really isn't his, you can't just say, "Look on the bright side of things. At least, you don't have to pay child support for the next 18 years." How insensitive! Or imagine someone's telling you after you've lost three family members that "at least you have some family left."

People mean well when they try to help others by saying something positive. But if the timing isn't right, it's not going to work. We may even be viewed as rude or insensitive. I've seen it happen dozens of times. Maybe you've even caught yourself saying things like this to others, but if the tables were turned, you might very well be pushed further down by the helpful advice.

A group of friends were hanging around, and one person in the group started to cry. No one knew what was wrong. I started to walk toward her to see if there was anything I could do to help. Before I got to her a lady, whom we'll call Beth, walked up to her and put her arm around her and asked what was wrong. I could overhear the lady who was crying say in response that someone in her family had recently died. Beth, meaning well, said, "You can get over it. My son died and I was able to move on."

A perfect illustration of bad timing. That statement might have helped at a later time if the grieving woman had asked if it's possible to get over such pain, but at the moment she was only beginning to deal with her loss. Timing is everything. What should Beth have said? Probably nothing. A good long, sincere hug would have been a lot more effective. We need care and consoling, not trite sayings. In time, we will be able to move on.

In the previous sentence, there is a very interesting clue about the healing process. It was the word "time." Every day, you hear people say, "Time heals all wounds." I agree that there is some truth in this statement, but it's far from a complete thought. I don't know about you, but if I had to wait on time to heal all the wounds that I've experienced, I'd still be bleeding to this day.

I've actually found the following statement to be far more helpful and enlightening when I'm trying to help someone. Time doesn't heal all wounds, you do.

If I had to wait on time to heal all the wounds that I've experienced, I'd still be bleeding to this day.

We have the choice to let time heal our wounds, but that doesn't give any control, and it doesn't always work. Another problem is that, for time to heal your wounds, you have to wait. If you had a painful experience in the past that was blocking you from present-day happiness or stopping you from increasing your income, would you rather get over that hurdle as soon as you can? Or would you be willing to wait for time to heal the wounds (whenever time gets around to it)? Most people would agree that it's far more satisfying, empowering, and fulfilling to be in control and deciding our direction in life, as opposed to letting things happen to us.

The method of healing your own wounds and not waiting on time may not be easy to apply. This is because, for everything you want out of life you must give up something. Your ability to heal your own wounds depends on how much of this something you are willing to give up.

The something in this case is comfort. It's making the decision to take the more difficult path in order to move beyond your present circumstances. Instead of letting life simply carry you along, you can decide to overcome the pain of a loss and to force the healing, which would normally happen over time, to happen more quickly. This frequently means moving beyond your comfort zone. It means refusing to wait for time to pass in order for healing to happen.

Your ability to heal your own wounds depends on how much of this something you are willing to give up.

If you think of this healing in direct comparison to a flesh wound, there are many parallels. In time, almost any nonfatal flesh wound will heal. The really bad ones take more time than the small scrapes. Sometimes, to treat a critical wound, you must endure a bit more short-term pain and crying while the doctor cleans the wound and sutures it. Ultimately, however, a treated wound will heal faster and more completely with less scarring than if you simply tried to ignore the injury.

Even people who understand this analogy may not know what the prescribed treatment should be, so they just let time do its thing. In practically every case, you must let time help you get past the initial shock of your tragedy or loss. However, once you pass the initial shock, you can begin to take control and speed your own healing process.

Unaided, some people take years to move on. They let their past rent space in their head for years. Some even take it to their graves with them.

You have a personal choice as to how much time you will allow to pass before you start taking the aggressive approach you are about to learn. Your personality, mind-set, and attitude will determine the speed of your process. If you haven't adopted a proactive mind-set, you may want to read the entire book before you try to begin forcing the following technique on yourself. That's because the last two chapters of this book will give you stories about what it's like to master your own circumstances and truly take control. I wish I had known how to take control and move on the way I do now. I thought (like most people) that the best answer is just to power through the hard times.

Your personality, mind-set, and attitude will determine the speed of your process.

I recall some of my mental bouts after going through all the things I did. The depression was like nothing I had ever experienced. I had days of constant crying, and I couldn't imagine how I could move on. I couldn't keep a steady relationship for the life of me. I was consumed with self-doubt, and if I felt a girlfriend was going to break up with me, I would lose it. In looking back, even I am amazed that I finally made it.

One of my major challenges was learning to handle any type of rejection, and not just in relationships; my problems affected my business life too. As I started various businesses,

I exposed myself to a tremendous amount of rejection. I know now that this is a necessary part of any entrepreneurial venture, but I wanted all the gain without the risk. I worked to earn as much as I could, and then I invested large sums of money in a new business venture, only to have the whole thing fall apart. The moment I felt something had failed, I would immediately remember all the other pain of my past. Every one of the failures and troubles in my past seemed to conspire to hit me all at once, business related or not. That's a lot of pain for one person to handle. That made it even harder to keep going. I kept thinking, if I am destined to keep failing, and each failure just brings up all my other failures, I had better quit soon, because I don't know if I can take any more pain.

POWER TIP

Words are simply perception. Your perception is a choice.

Ultimately, you have to deal with past pains because there will come a time when you can no longer just power through. I liken it to snow on the roof of a building. Buildings are built with strong roofs. They are designed to handle snow. Nevertheless, the snow builds up. If it's not removed, it starts getting heavier and heavier. Eventually, the roof will cave in. Our emotions can be that way as well. The more painful the past, the more snow you have on the roof. I'm not interested in discovering how strong my roof is. When I get snow on my roof, I start shoveling before it gets too heavy. Dealing proactively with negative things from your past is like shoveling and reinforcing your roof, all at the same time.

So how much time should you let pass—in order to get beyond the initial pain of a problem—before you take control and change circumstances in order to move on?

Dealing proactively with negative things from your past is like shoveling and reinforcing your roof, all at the same time.

We've all heard our parents preach the following adage: "When you fall off the horse, get right back on it." We've all heard this before, and we've all told each other to do it. When we say, "Get right back on the horse," we mean right away. Don't wait. But what makes it so difficult to get back on the horse now? It's because you are still feeling the emotional or physical pain. Getting back on the horse right now seems to be too much, too soon. But what's the payoff if we do manage to get right back on the horse anyway? We master the situation, and we don't let it rent space in our head. Waiting to get back on the horse a week or months from now doesn't usually help. If anything, the longer we wait the more intense the fear we will develop. This will only serve to make it that much harder to get back on the horse.

The old adage speaks of horses, though. I'm not saying if your spouse dies, start dating the next day. Or if you've invested a lot of money in something and it fails, dump more in immediately. There needs to be a time to feel the pain, but how long you need to feel this pain before you move forward is up to you. And I want you to notice that I won't tell you what specific time frame is right. It depends on your personality and the circumstances, and everyone is different.

I'm always intrigued when people respond judgmentally when someone remarries quickly after the death of a spouse or following a divorce.

I won't tell you what specific time frame is right. It depends on your personality and the circumstances, and everyone is different.

How long should a person wait? Nine months? A year and a half? What's the right answer? How about 14 months, 2 weeks, and 3 days. Silly isn't it? Why should it be our business? It shouldn't matter if the people involved are able to move on. If they can truly move on quickly, then great for them! It's important to understand that people who think that the hurt person may be moving on too quickly may be imposing their own time frame on the situation. Maybe if they moved on that quickly, they would still be on the rebound, and it would be a bad move. If the involved person has moved past the point of risking a rebound relationship, regardless of how little time has passed, then moving on is exactly what that person should do.

For me personally, I usually want to move on as quickly as I can, but let me break that down a little. I'm not talking about starting a new relationship right away. I just wanted to get over my divorce so I could be ready for the possibility of a new relationship as quickly as possible. As for business, I want to march forcefully forward as quickly as I can, while making sure I'm headed in a profitable, promising direction.

When you are in a very depressed, discouraged, or negative state it's hard to adopt this attitude unless you have committed to this course mentality before it all hits the fan. Planning ahead like this must be a way of life. Otherwise, it would be like trying to learn to swim when you're drowning. Not the best time to take lessons or try to be self-taught. Some people reading this book may be drowning now. Instead of trying to move on quickly right now, take the time to read the whole book, and use some of the little techniques as a life preserver. Make it to shore, and rest a little, so that you learn from the past and deal with the future with a more prepared mind-set.

I mentioned that I wanted to move past the pain of my ex-wife, and because personal tragedies are frequently more difficult to overcome than business failures, at least on a deep, emotional level, I had to do some pretty challenging things to get over my divorce. As you read the following story, you'll realize that if you want to try something like this, it will be a lot easier said than done, but in the end, I assure you the trouble was well worth it for me.

I started with the belief that we need to feel the pain, but to try not to wallow in it forever. I married young (at 17) and had a business with employees during my last year of high school. My wife cheated on me with one of my employees for three years, and it started when he was just 15! Imagine what that will do to your ego. Then, of course, matters got worse when I found out the baby we had wasn't even mine. The pain was incredibly intense. I had started my second business and was making over one hundred thousand dollars a year as a teenager. I happened to be my family's first generation jeweler and did quite well until all this happened.

After losing everything, I couldn't function emotionally. I drank and cried myself to sleep for months. I finally came to the point that I had to come up with a way to move on, but I wanted to do it faster because time wasn't healing my wounds quickly enough. My problems had ruined me financially, and they were taking their toll on me emotionally. I was determined to take control and heal all my wounds! The only thing I could hang on to was the memory of my business success, because I was sure that was real. Even though my businesses were gone, I used my business approach as a starting point for my plan. I would make a business out of overcoming my personal, emotional pain.

I had discovered the places where my ex had cheated on me. I couldn't even drive near them. The mental pictures, the pain—it was all too intense. Problem number one: Every time I avoided driving by these areas, I was rewarding my negative feelings, because I didn't want to feel the pain. Enough was enough. I knew that I was done letting pain control me.

I purposely drove to the locations I had avoided and cried my eyes out. I did it day after day—not to drown in my tears but to get the pain out of my system. The most important part of doing something like this is the right attitude. Without the right attitude, you are just reliving the pain and the mental pictures. My attitude was this, *I've got to move on. Let me expe-*

rience the pain so I'm not controlled by it any more. So I cried and cried. It was a mental and emotional cleansing for me. Now I can drive by those same places and not be controlled by memories. Didn't it still hurt for a long time? Sure. It's part of being human. But the pain doesn't own me anymore.

Another piece of the puzzle is that you need hope to overcome great challenges or tragedy. People who are clinically depressed due to a brain chemical imbalance may well need professional help in modifying their brain chemistry before they are ready for change. Their minds can't even comprehend hope, so that they can use the hope as a basis for action and use other tools in order to get past their troubles. Although phobias aren't usually chemically induced, they often are related to extremely bad wiring of the brain. The victim needs professional help there as well.

Some minimal shred of hope must exist as a starting motivation to use other tools or techniques such as Attitude Adjusting Statements, pushing to feel as much pain in a brief period as possible, staying busy, or simply the passage of time. If hope exists, you can use these tools and others to move ahead forcefully and purposefully in your life. If you have hope you can take control.

Frequently hope is a God-given gift, but you can also generate it for yourself (especially in business if you plan ahead), and others can help you feel more hope too.

If hope exists, you can use these tools and others to move ahead forcefully and purposefully in your life.

I recall, many years ago, getting a phone call about an older friend of mine named Andrew. The caller told me that Andrew, in his eighties at the time, had been sent to the hospital and only had a few days to live. My wife and I, with another couple, decided to go to the hospital to visit him before he died. As we walked into his hospital room, I could see all the flowers and get well cards. Within 30 seconds of being there Andrew looked at me and said, "I just want to die." My heart fell. Now everyone is looking at me as if to say, *Okay, Gary, you're the guy with the words, say something.*

Because of Andrew's frame of mind, I knew anything I could say to him would be like positive thinking. In this setting, positive thinking is like spray paint on rust. When someone says, "I wish I were dead," he has obviously lost all hope and purpose. The typical helpful rapid-fire comments like "but you've got your friends," "look at all these cards and flowers you have," "God loves you," "your family loves you"—comments like these are just positive thinking and will even push someone in a hopeless state further away. They also communicate that you just don't get it or understand.

As I left his hospital room, I must admit, I felt a bit helpless myself. All I could say was "Andrew, hang in there!" Anything more would just be spray paint on rust.

The next day, I received another phone call. This time, the caller told me that Andrew had been sent home, because that's where he had chosen to die. I don't know what it was about that call but a light went on inside my head, and I thought I had come up with a way to give Andrew some hope and purpose.

Four of us went to Andrew's house and went to work! We cleaned the toilets, we cleaned the kitchen, and at some point I walked past his room. As fragile as he was, Andrew straightened up in his bed. He had tears in his eyes, and he said, "I never realized that people cared."

Now, I was thinking, *What you are talking about?! You have all these flowers and get well cards. What do you mean you didn't realize that people cared?!*

You see, sending flowers and cards is the proper thing to do, but it can be meaningless to some people when it's expected. For whatever reason, we chose to do something unexpected. The fact that this was a different display of caring seemed to reach Andrew on a level he hadn't experienced from the cards and flowers. It was the thing he needed to realize people really *did* care. In the frame of mind he shared at the hospital, we could have told him 10,000 times, "Don't you realize that people care? Don't you realize that we care?" Words like that were what he expected, and we both knew they wouldn't have changed anything.

My friends and I decided to show Andrew that we cared in a different way, and we cared for years after this. We occasionally stopped by and fixed things in his house, and he loved the attention and visits. His hope was alive and well. It's kind of funny, but we reasoned, if we cleaned the inside of Andrew's house and he lived happily for several more years, imagine what would happen if we cleaned the outside of his house. After a couple of years, about 15 or 20 of us painted, cleaned, and beautified the outside, and Andrew did live for several more years.

Was it the clean house that helped Andrew's recovery? No, he recovered because his hope and his purpose were back. This kind of drive from having a purpose in life can get you up in the morning. Look for the things you add to those sharing the planet with you. How do you improve the lives you touch? Are there special gifts you share?

I encourage you to find these special things in life and business, and when you think you've found enough, find some more. You can never have enough hope or purpose. They make your life full and rich. Another advantage of doing all this is that inevitably something bad will happen to you. The more purpose and hope you have in life, the quicker you'll usually bounce back.

Let's talk about hope in business. One of my good friends told me that this is his favorite lesson from my seminars. The concept is that, in business, the more projects you have going, the more hope you have. If one of your projects goes bust or falls through, you still have all your other avenues to pursue, and one of them is sure to pay off.

My friend is an entrepreneur, and he had been in his business for years. He was usually doing fine with occasional ups and downs, but he never seemed to break through to the next level. He was almost always in a good mood and had a positive outlook, but he always seemed to be at the mercy of a poorly paying client or waiting to see if some big project was going to pay off. Every time one of his big projects fizzled, it would take him weeks or even months to get back on track financially.

In business, the more projects you have going, the more hope you have. If one of your projects goes bust or falls through, you still have all your other avenues to pursue, and one of them is sure to pay off.

He dropped by one of my seminars, as he did from time to time, and he was familiar with nearly all of the lessons I taught. For some reason, that day he focused on the business idea that more projects means more hope, and he started to brainstorm all the little projects he could adapt his business to pursue.

Inside three weeks he had begun work on more little projects than he had ever started at once. None of the projects had yet panned out, but his normally positive mood was through the roof. I asked him if he was in a good mood because his latest big business plan had worked, and he said that wasn't the reason. He was in such a great mood and busier than ever because he had so many things going that one (or more) of them was sure to pay off.

He was prospecting for new clients in ways he had never pursued before. At the same time, he was developing new products and services to deliver to a wider audience. He was trying all kinds of things, and, in the long run, the ones that paid off big had been on his back burner for years. He was always waiting until one of his big projects paid off, so that he would have the free time to pursue this other little project. His business cycle changed from big ups and downs to constant, steady growth on a big scale. The idea that the more projects you pursue, the more hope you feel had helped him balance his workload, and when one of his projects didn't go as planned, he still had all kinds of hope, because of the many other things that he had going. His hope and his attitude were fine tuned to keep him moving forward.

Attitude is so important, and we must use concepts like these to develop a strong one before we need it. When tough times happen, they can wreak havoc on your attitude. If you don't have a good attitude to begin with, you're going to need to learn to swim real fast.

Positive thinking by itself has long been an answer suggested by pop psychologists and pushed by well-meaning friends to help people get through tough times, but it's just a small piece of the big puzzle. Things like attitude, timing, and hope all figure into a person's ability to get to the positive thinking phase.

Attitude is so important, and we must use concepts like these to develop a strong one before we need it.

In this chapter and the pages that follow, I have provided a host of tools you can use to get through tough times or to move from wherever you are to the next level. I hope that positive thinking will always be a part of your life, because you understand its place in the bigger picture, not because it seems to be an answer in and of itself.

Take some time to consider all the ways you touch others' lives and anything that gives you hope on a personal level. Consider what you are doing in business, and think about additional things you might do to improve your company's position if current projects don't go as planned or to branch out to attract more clients and additional streams of income. And while you're thinking about these things, keep in mind that you are laying the foundation, so that you can have an attitude that will help you be resilient when the tough times come. You'll be able to respond more quickly, regain control, and keep moving forward. Even though positive thinking may be part of your plan, you won't have to wait for time to heal your wounds or positive thinking to fix things. You're more powerful than that now.

SUMMARY

- Positive thinking alone solves nothing.
- Positive thinking doesn't fix the underlying problem. It's like spray paint on rust, and it won't last long.
- Positive affirmations are equally ineffective.
- Positive thinking is only occasionally effective as an ingredient in a bigger recipe for pulling your life together.
- Timing influences the effectiveness of positive thinking.
- Time doesn't heal all wounds, you do.
- Your personality, mind-set, and attitude will determine the speed of your process.
- You can choose to do whatever it takes to get over business and personal challenges as quickly as possible but . . . when you are in a very depressed, discouraged or negative state, it's hard to adopt this attitude, unless you have committed to this mentality before all your troubles hit the fan.
- Hope is a key element in the ability to move on.
- Frequently, hope comes naturally, but if it seems to be missing, you can generate it for yourself (especially in

business if you plan ahead), and others can help you feel more hope too.

- In business, the more projects you have going, the more hope you have. If one of your projects goes bust or falls through, you still have all your other avenues to pursue, and one of them is sure to pay off.
- Positive thinking has its place, and in that way it's a good thing. But it's never an answer by itself.

Chapter 8

MENTAL VERTIGO— DO YOU HAVE IT?

It was an unfortunate accident that caught the entire country off guard. Three young, active, well-known people—JFK, Jr., his wife, and her sister—died in a plane crash. After studying the crash, FAA investigators determined that the cause of the accident was the pilot's failure to maintain orientation. Additionally, they concluded that the disorientation was strongly influenced by marginal weather.

JFK, Jr., got into what pilots refer to as "vertigo." Maybe you've heard of vertigo. Physicians use the term to describe dizziness or disorientation. In flying, it means something else. It's not necessarily dizziness, although that may be involved. Vertigo is any disorientation from environmental factors that cause you to believe that the attitude of your plane is something other than what it truly is. It's usually deadly when you make decisions based on your senses (vision, balance, and so forth), which provide incorrect or inadequate information. Studies show that inexperienced pilots will crash within three minutes if they fly into certain marginal weather situations for which they have not been trained.

In aviation, there are various training levels or certifications you can achieve. Initially, someone will start taking lessons to earn a Private Pilots License (PPL). This is a great start into aviation (although there are other paths into aviation). Next, many new pilots purchase or rent a plane and are allowed to fly to another state or even another country. With respect to the basic PPL, perhaps the biggest restriction associated with this certification is the various weather conditions in which pilots are permitted to fly. The law states that PPL holders must stay clear of clouds or storms, and in most cases they need at least three miles of visibility.

It's usually deadly when you make decisions based on your senses (vision, balance, and so forth), which provide incorrect or inadequate information.

A pilot with a private rating flies according to Visual Flight Rules (VFRs). That's why the limitation is placed on them to fly only in good weather and when visibility is good. Their ability to navigate in a manner that relies heavily on visual cues means that, if they fly in a cloud they not only can't see, they are breaking the law. When VFR-rated pilots fly in marginal weather, they have to be very aware of developing conditions and the distance to visual impairments in order to continue to fly both legally and safely. The danger lies in inexperienced pilots trying to push the limits of their experience and training, especially in marginal or low-visibility situations.

You may think it's obvious why this is so dangerous, but think a little further. Without any visual reference, the only way you can know where you are going and what the airplane is doing is to rely completely on the instruments in the cockpit. Without proper training, practically everyone will begin to ignore the instruments and fly by instinct. If you've ever flown, even as a passenger on a large jet, you know that clouds frequently make for a bumpy ride. Small planes experience the same rough ride through clouds. As you bounce around in the airplane, the fluid in your inner ear begins to move, which in turn cause spatial disorientation. Up may become down, left might feel like right and so on. If you enter a turbulent airstream with limited or zero visibility, it is simply impossible to use the senses you normally would depend on to accurately judge your orientation.

POWER TIP

For every positive thing you experience in your life, there are a million other people experiencing the same thing and hating it. For every negative thing you experience in your life, there are a million other people experiencing the exact same thing and loving it.

> *Without proper training, practically everyone will begin to ignore the instruments and fly by instinct.*

Unfortunately, to this day pilots still crash because they get into mental vertigo. Often, a pilot who is not properly trained or rated will depart in marginal weather, and the weather starts to deteriorate during the flight. Instead of landing or turning around, the pilot pushes it, keeps going, and gets socked in. Without sufficient training or experience flying by instruments alone, a pilot may end up flying into a mountain or crashing nose first while believing the plane is in straight and level flight.

Life is often like this. One moment, we feel sure about our success, and the next moment that feeling of success we had just a day ago, or even five minutes ago, is no longer there.

Although I speak to seminar audiences regularly, the topics aren't always the same. Sometimes, I have an opportunity to include an explanation of mental vertigo as part of my program. To make my illustration more powerful, I ask the audience to hold their right arm straight out in front of them with their hand flat and palm facing the ground to represent a plane in straight and level flight. Next, I have them point the thumb of their right hand to the seven o'clock position to represent a smooth, banking turn to the left. I ask them to keep their palm in this left turn position for a minute as I continue the explanation.

One moment, we feel sure about our success, and the next moment that feeling of success we had just a day ago, or even five minutes ago, is no longer there.

I say, "Imagine that you are flying along, and all of a sudden you get caught in bad weather. The plane shakes and clouds obscure your vision. Remember, don't move your hand from the left banking turn."

I continue, "Now imagine that you've been bounced around for a few minutes and you still don't have visual cues to help you reorient yourself. If your *feelings* told you that you were banking to the right—and look at your hand, you're still banking left—so if your *feelings* told you that you were banking right and you wanted to correct the plane to establish a left bank (in order to fly level) what would that mean?"

As I have the audience move their hand to indicate a further left turn, many of them even lean left as the tops of their outstretched hands start facing the ground and their palms begin turning upward. The original left bank that you had initiated, coupled with your *feeling* that you were banking right as a result of mental vertigo, has caused you to roll to the left even further. Now you are upside down, and you are totally out of control. That's the deadly reality of vertigo.

At this point, people who don't have any experience flying, and even some VFR private pilots, ask, "But why don't you just fly by the instruments? That should be easy. The instruments tell you exactly what to do." Although this is very true, an untrained person, no matter how smart or quick she is, will not make it. Your feelings have guided you all your life, and the drive to obey your feelings is stronger than your logical mind's ability to reason through the situation and use the instruments. As a VFR-rated pilot with little or no exposure to instrument flying, JFK, Jr., must have had precisely this sort of trouble.

A number of lessons can be learned here. First is the difference between flying by your feelings and flying by your instruments. The more risk you take in business and in life, the more susceptible you will be to mental vertigo. Taking risks and pushing past your own personal comfort zone can cause a rough ride, and that's the beginning of mental vertigo. So if we don't learn to master mental vertigo, we'll tailspin and crash.

Although this is very true, an untrained person, no matter how smart or quick she is, will not make it. Your feelings have guided you all your life, and the drive to obey your feelings is stronger than your logical mind's ability to reason through the situation and use the instruments.

There's even more to instrument flying than you might imagine. By law, your instruments must be calibrated at regular intervals. Imagine flying in bad weather with a full complement of instruments. You've been trained to fly by your instruments, so you're ready to go. What if you haven't kept them calibrated? This is sure to spell disaster. Instrument training is only part of the picture, because if some of your instruments are off just a few degrees, the error could mean the difference between landing on a runway and crashing into a mountain, a radio tower, or a building.

Another thing a private pilot must do before being permitted to fly in bad weather or clouds is to get enough additional training to earn an additional certification. The next license for many pilots is to attain an instrument rating. That way they can fly IFR (Instrument Flight Rules). For pilots to go from a private pilot's license to an instrument rating/license, they must spend a minimum of (approximately) 40 additional hours practicing instrument-only flying with a qualified instrument instructor.

The majority of the training actually consists of actual flying in good weather, but you *pretend* that you are flying in zero visibility weather. This is done by making the student wear a hood or foggles (fog-simulating goggles). You put the hood on like a hat, but the hood protrudes from the front about 8 inches or so, and is curved on the left and right side so that you can't see outside the cockpit. It's like flying with blinders on, because you can only see the instruments on the panel in front of you. The hood also blocks the view through the windshield so that the pilot can't see out at all. This is called simulated instrument training because external conditions don't require instrument use. This kind of instrument flying makes up most of the logged hours pilots use toward qualifying for an instrument rating. After meeting the hourly qualifications and becoming proficient in specific maneuvers, the candidate takes a check-ride with an FAA examiner who confirms the candidate's ability to meet prescribed standards. After logging sufficient hours with a certified instructor and passing the check-ride, the pilot gets an IFR rating and is allowed to fly through clouds and in most bad weather.

In life and business, if we are not properly trained and prepared for the hard times, the challenging times will cause us to go into mental vertigo, and we'll be in trouble. Trust me, troubled times will come. The more experience you gain in dealing with these problems or challenges, the more you can handle them, and the better equipped you will be to handle additional challenges in the future.

If we are not properly trained and prepared for the hard times, the challenging times will cause us to go into mental vertigo, and we'll be in trouble.

I'd like to give you a preview of what you'll be doing later in order to identify your instruments, calibrate them, and begin to fly by them. First you'll identify what your beliefs are. You need to determine if your beliefs will get you desired results or if they're keeping you back or even causing you problems. Do your beliefs help you, your company, or both? Or are your beliefs putting you or your company in danger?

You'll also need to understand how to calibrate your beliefs (instruments), and you don't just set 'em and forget 'em. You need a regular schedule of training and calibration to keep you and your equipment in top form. For example, as an instrument pilot, I am required by law to execute a specific number of approaches, simulated or real. An approach is basically a pilot's method for flying into a landing pattern at an airport without seeing it from a distance. You must rely strictly on your instruments to get to the airport. Every six months, the FAA wants you to make sure you are on top of your game by logging several instrument approaches. If you go beyond the six-month limit, you must fly with an instructor to practice these approaches. These strict guidelines even apply to a pilot like me who has been flying for years.

You need a regular schedule of training and calibration to keep you and your equipment in top form.

Now when you consider the effects of vertigo and the training necessary to teach someone to ignore feelings and obey instruments, it might just sound as though the FAA has appropriately strict guidelines in place. Here is something that is very interesting, though. Do you realize that many, if not most, pilots who pass their instrument check-ride, *who are legal to fly in the clouds and take you up with them,* have never actually flown through a cloud? Did you know that most have little or no experience actually flying in weather where you have to rely solely on the instruments?

Here is something that's even scarier. The flight instructor who trained the new IFR pilot may not have been through that kind of real-world experience either. That's right. Many people become flight instructors because it helps them build more flying hours, which is a requirement to get hired by major airlines. (Students pay them while they build time.) If they do have some actual experience flying in instruments-only weather, it's unusual to find someone who has as much as 10 or 20 hours doing it.

You can actually get your instrument rating and then move on to becoming an instrument-rated flight instructor, give other pilots (your students) the necessary training and instruction so they can pass their instrument check ride, and do this for years, while never actually experiencing instrument flying conditions yourself. This is all totally legal!

Now I didn't tell you all that to make you afraid to fly. Most commercial pilots have more hours in clouds than pilots with just an IFR rating have in planes. The point here is that credentials are one thing, experience is another.

I'd like you to consider one more thing. I don't intend to suggest that all people who are flight instructors without in-cloud experience are bad teachers, but wouldn't you think that the ones with more zero-visibility flying under their belt would generally make better instructors? If that's true, it may help you to remember that I have navigated through some of the roughest storms life can throw at you, and what I tell you is based on what I've learned about instrument flying from having been there. If something I tell you doesn't sound like what you'd hear from a Ph.D., that might just be because my examples and my tools come from in-cloud time and not from a text book.

With flight ratings, the good thing is that most FAA examiners understand that the rating doesn't mean the pilot is experienced. As a result, many examiners will give new IFR pilots a stern warning about using their new rating slowly. The best approach is to take time and gain experience in marginal conditions instead of pushing the limits of your newly earned certification. You fly, you learn. You fly more, you learn more. You build up your confidence and you determine what your limitations are and then stay within them until you build more experience and so on.

A seasoned pilot will begin to rely more on his instruments and less on his feelings. When a pilot feels or experiences vertigo but totally ignores his feelings and flies strictly by what his instruments tell him, he has mastered vertigo.

It's inevitable that in life we are going to experience mental vertigo. We just get that feeling at times that we can't figure out up from down or left from right. What should we do when that happens? Well, what do pilots do? They immediately fly by their instruments. You must do the same.

Keep in mind, the time to identify your beliefs and try to fly by them is *not* while you're in the clouds or bad weather. Consider this book as flight training for life to assist you in flying by your own beliefs (instruments), and to make sure they are properly calibrated.

SUMMARY

▌ People move forward based on their interpretation of where they *think* they are right now.

▌ If where you *think* you are is different from reality, you may be headed in the wrong direction altogether.

▌ Pilots learn to fly by their instruments and ignore their feelings.

▌ With proper training you can do this in business and life too.

▌ When things get hectic personally or professionally your feelings can put you in a tailspin, but if you're trained to pay attention to your beliefs, they can act as your instruments to guide you through the tough times.

▌ You must learn how to fly by your beliefs before you enter the storm.

Chapter 9

BEWARE OF THE
MARATHON RUNNER
WHO SMILES

Success hurts. Usually not in the end but along the way, the journey to your goal will almost always have a measure of painful experiences. The truth is, life is tough. Life's not fair. Achievement can be a battle. Self-help books and experts who tell you that the act of setting a goal will put you on autopilot toward success are oversimplifying.

This isn't just a feel-good book that just glosses over the tough times. This book is about triumph in spite of the tough times and being able to move ahead and not let other people or other things rent space in your head. People lose credibility when they tell you success and reaching your goals is easy, when it's not. Great achievement is inevitably the result of dealing with great challenges, and people get discouraged when they look to role models who have achieved success and who seem to be living the good life. So many times people think, *It's not supposed to be this hard.* They're wrong.

People lose credibility when they tell you success and reaching your goals is easy, when it's not.

I have worked with thousands of people who want to be more successful or overcome some major life challenge, and frequently they have one or more of the following beliefs. Unfortunately, these beliefs are suggested as a simple formula for success or an excuse for not achieving it, but each one is an outrageous lie. These beliefs won't serve you, and they almost always lead to failure:

- Successful people are all lucky.
- Dreams can come true if you believe in them.
- Just set a goal, and it will happen.
- Positive thinking solves problems.
- I just don't have what it takes.
- I'm not old enough yet (or I'm too old).
- It takes too much money to do what I want.
- I'm realistic, big success will never happen for me.
- I'm not talented enough.
- I don't have any free time to do that.
- You have to know the right people, and I don't have any connections.
- I can't find any mentors.
- I'm too fat.
- I had a bad childhood.
- My parents were alcoholics.
- I just can't get motivated.
- I'm not good at business.

- I had a bad divorce.
- I can't control my _____ (eating, emotions, drinking, and so forth).
- My mind doesn't work that way.
- I don't have that type of personality.
- I'm too tired.
- There aren't any jobs.
- I've already tried everything.
- Nothing I do ever works anyway, why bother?
- It's just not meant to be.
- I wouldn't even know where to start.
- I'm not that lucky.
- It would take too much time.
- I already work hard enough as it is.
- Nobody understands me.
- I can't do it by myself, I'd need a whole team to make that happen.
- I'm afraid of failing.
- I don't have the Midas Touch.
- Running a marathon is easy, just smile through the pain.

What a crock! These are a bunch of out-and-out lies we tell ourselves! Every one of these statements is an excuse to avoid trying. I bet you could write a chapter for every one of these excuses people use, why they're wrong, and what the real truth is. I'm confident the audience reading this book is emotionally mature enough to see the holes in each of these absurd excuses, so I won't bore you with the reasons why each excuse is a waste of your time.

Every one of these statements is an excuse to avoid trying.

I speak from experience when I say success is great! Reaching big goals is incredible! Success is worth the effort! But success is *not* painless, and it's *never* easy all along the way. Part of what makes success so rewarding is the struggle to reach your goal. Reaching a business or personal goal is rewarding because of the limited number of people who can achieve at that level. Most people just get caught up in the drudgery of daily life or bogged down by their own crummy excuse-ridden beliefs. And then their limiting beliefs about their own handicaps to success are reinforced by the media's portrayal of successful people— smiling, jet-setting, luxury lifestyles with no hint of the struggles it took to get to the good life, or what it takes to maintain that level of success. I've produced a CD series entitled *Secrets That My Millionaire Mentors Taught Me About Business and Success*. The series is full of interviews with amazingly successful people, whose companies make hundreds of millions, and others billions, annually. And my goal is to avoid pulling punches and just showing the stereotypical, infomercial view of success. As you listen to them speak from the heart and from the gut, you'll hear about the hard times along the way—because that's reality.

POWER TIP

Are you willing to pay the price? Most say they are, but even more don't even know what the price is.

Granted, most of us haven't run a 26.2-mile marathon, but this chapter will still make sense. Those who *have* run a marathon certainly have learned a tremendous amount about themselves and the mind games that they play with themselves during their run.

> *My goal is to avoid pulling punches and just showing the stereotypical, infomercial view of success.*

Even if you don't know anyone personally who has run a marathon, I'm sure you know that no one ever just wakes up and says, "I hear there is a marathon next week, I'm going to enter it." Preparing for a marathon takes months of physical and mental conditioning. Someone might start off with running a mile or two (if he can make it that far). Then he has to let his body heal and adjust to the exercise regimen, especially if he's new to running. After some time, he works up to five, and 10, and 20 miles.

Any time I've ever watched a marathon, I don't recall the runners having big, happy grins on their faces and chanting trite, positive affirmations. In fact, immediately after the finish line, lots of runners collapse. I even remember seeing runners literally crawl to the finish line in tears. You just have to admire the fact that they finished. They crossed the finish line. That was their goal, and they made it.

We must remember that it can be very painful to even try to cross our personal finish line. This is why we have to focus on the end at the beginning and develop our plan for getting there. We always have a choice to keep running or quit.

I remember a time in my young life when I didn't have enough money to buy groceries. That's a real humbling experience. That didn't bring a smile to my face, nor did I want someone to tell me to just smile or think positive. In spite of all the hardships along the way, and the temptation to quit, I kept running. During the really tough times, it may be impossible to put on a smile and look at the bright side of things. Regardless, if you have a plan to reach your goal, you've got to keep moving. Even if you're moving slow, you're still moving.

We have to focus on the end at the beginning and develop our plan for getting there.

I often hear people say, "Just smile." This usually tells me that they aren't in touch with my destination or my current struggles. Would a seasoned marathon runner who is running alongside you at the 17th mile, when you are thinking about quitting, say, "Smile, it's not that bad"?

No way. He or she would probably tell you to keep going and don't give up. Things are tough, that's true. Stay focused. Stick to your plan. Remember the finish line is your goal. And the seasoned runner wouldn't be smiling either. If there's a self-proclaimed marathon runner in your life who tells you to smile while you're in pain, he probably hasn't run many marathons, if any. Oh, it would be nice to smile all the time, but that isn't reality. Big goals yield big challenges, and sometimes smiling just wastes your energy and makes you lose sight of your plan and your finish line. When you're in the thick of a battle, it may be all you can do to simply focus on your plan.

And don't think that the little *life isn't fair—there will be struggles—get a grip, this is reality* chapter is an excuse to be rude or harsh or grumpy whenever you're working on your goals. It's not. You still need to be nice to everybody else on the playground. It's just that, during times of true struggle, it's not practical to try to smile all the time.

The tool you can use to keep going through rough times is to make sure you work your plan. The marathon runner, although feeling pain and exhaustion at times in the race, still puts one foot in front of another. That's his or her plan. That really is the key. The goal is the finish line, and the plan is one foot in front of the other. Focus on the plan, not the pain.

What's your plan? Every goal must have a plan. When things aren't going our way, we don't need to smile to make it through. Don't give in to your desire to quit. Don't believe the lies of those who suggest success is easy. Just focus on your plan, and keep chipping away at it. If the struggle slows you down, keep chipping. Pride yourself in being able to have things fall apart all around you but somehow still bounce back and keep chipping away at your plan. No matter how slow you may be at times, keep putting one foot in front of the other. *Just don't quit.*

Don't believe the lies of those who suggest success is easy. Just focus on your plan, and keep chipping away at it.

What would you think of a person who told you that she was a marathon runner, and you found out that every time she only ran about five miles and quit? Sure, she is all excited and smiling when she starts. She has the right shirt, shorts, and shoes. She looks the part. She pours on the power at the beginning of the race and then starts hurting. She tries hard to look like a successful runner, but she never finishes a race. Then, she gets all excited about the next marathon and signs

POWER TIP

No is an acceptable answer.

up, only to do the same thing again. What if you found out this pattern had been going on for years? This person is a wannabe marathoner.

Too often, I see people get started on a goal, and because they get to a painful threshold they look for a better path or an easier way. They never finish what they start, but they keep starting something new because there seems to be an easier way and they're struggling. It happens in business. It happens in relationships. If we want to reach the finish line of our goals, if we want to experience real success, we must accept the fact that pain is going to be a part of the process.

We've all been told that you must love what you do. I am a firm believer in that. Unfortunately, some people take that concept too literally. They think that loving what you do means always enjoying everything about what you do all the time you're doing it. That's simply unrealistic. Yes, we should love what we do, but that doesn't mean the goal we are pursuing is necessarily wrong if we experience a lot of pain while doing it. We should never automatically conclude that we need to switch gears because the process seems too painful.

If we want to experience real success, we must accept the fact that pain is going to be a part of the process.

Consider the biggest, most successful businesses and professionals you know. I guarantee they've struggled along the way. And they've probably been at it for years. Every athlete has pushed to be better and reach personal goals. Look at people who have been married for decades. They enjoy and love each other. But has it ever been painful? No question about it. It's the overall love that causes them to put one foot in front of the other during the tough times.

Anybody who tells you that you can run a marathon and smile all the way is lying. Life is tough. Life's not fair. You will struggle. You'll feel pain. Just keep working your plan because it's worth it in the end.

SUMMARY

▮ Big success is never painless.

▮ Part of what makes success so rewarding is the struggle to reach your goal.

▮ Too many TV shows and books say that success in love or business is easy if you know the formula. They're wrong.

Chapter 10

BE PREPARED TO ABORT OR LOSE AN ENGINE— THE POWER OF NEGATIVE THINKING

Throughout the last few chapters, we spent a lot of time exposing the flaws of traditional wisdom when it comes to self-improvement and making change for the better. By now you should understand, at least on an intellectual level, that positive thinking and irrational optimism often cause more harm than good. That's true.

Ironically, though, just because people may understand the hoax of positive thinking, that doesn't necessarily mean that they understand the *power* of *negative* thinking. The thought process usually runs something like this: *Okay, positive thinking won't fix things, and later in the book I'll learn strategies I can use to really overcome obstacles. Nevertheless, I should still probably try to avoid negative thoughts because they bring me down. Negative thoughts can't be good.* The truth is, that's wrong too.

Now it *is* true that negative *attitudes* can bring you down further, especially if you're already down. But thoughts and ideas that most people would consider negative can often be powerful and helpful. You need negative thoughts to be balanced in your life, and negative thoughts will help you along the way.

One of the reasons people try to avoid negative thoughts is because they have been told that focusing on the negative will cause those negative things to happen or they'll relive some painful experiences. And who wants to do that? It may be possible that a steadfast focus on *just* the negative might draw you toward negative results. That's the reason why most people don't enjoy spending lots of time with pessimists. But you can use thoughts about negative things (not negative attitudes) in order to keep bad things from happening. Negative thoughts can be tools for making good things happen.

Thoughts and ideas that most people would consider negative can often be powerful and helpful.

I've had a love of aviation from the time I was a little child. Almost every kid, from time to time, dreams of being able to fly, but I had an added incentive because my family had been involved in aviation for years. Ever since I can remember, I knew I wanted to learn to fly.

I've been flying now for over 20 years, and I've amassed numerous ratings. I am certified as an instructor for private, single-engine, and twin-engine airplanes, and for helicopters. I'm certified to teach people how to fly by their instruments, and I am even certified as a Captain on Learjets. Most people with this number of certifications have military experience, but I just love flying, so I took all this training on my own. And speaking of Learjets, that's a whole different ball game. I really thought I knew how to fly until I went to Learjet school.

Before stepping up into the cockpit of something as fast and sophisticated as a Learjet, most of my flying had been in smaller, light, single- and multiengine aircraft. Compared to driving a car, flying a plane is far more complicated, and you have to know and do many more things simultaneously. When you first tackle learning to fly, it can seem overwhelming, but even with the extra instruments, rules, and preflight considerations, most pilots eventually achieve a level of comfort with small planes. These days, I'd even consider training for this type of aircraft to be simple. By contrast, Learjets are quite a bit more complicated, and training is far more demanding. Things happen fast in a jet!

Compared to driving a car, flying a plane is far more complicated, and you have to know and do many more things simultaneously.

Because of this, small, private planes don't usually require simulator training, and most people get a license with no simulator training at all. These little planes are forgiving enough that a flight instructor can compensate for mistakes and correct problems during an actual flight with minimal risk. If you look hard, you might be able to find a small plane flight simulator, but it's obvious that they aren't anywhere near the level of sophistication you'll find in a full-motion Learjet simulator. A Learjet simulator can cost between $10 million and $20 million—more than the jet itself. But the training is priceless.

An added benefit I've realized as a result of my Learjet simulator time is that I can fly less-sophisticated aircraft with even more skill and caution. The reason is that simulator training is based on what-if scenarios. What if you lose an engine? What if your engine catches fire? What if you lose cabin pressure? What if your landing gear doesn't extend? And the list goes on. By the way, these simulators are so amazingly realistic, if you just spent time learning in a simulator, with professional instruction, and never set foot on an actual Learjet flight deck, you could literally fly a Learjet without any additional experience.

Learjet simulator training is almost never uneventful, sunny weather, problem-free aviation. As you're flying along in your full-size cockpit simulator, your instructor pushes a button behind you on a computer, and all of a sudden there's smoke in the cockpit. Not a *picture* of smoke on a computer screen, this is the actual stuff that floats in the air and interferes with vision. If that's not exciting enough, he pushes another button, and now your right engine is on fire. In a simulator, the fire isn't real, but with the smoke and beeping and flashing lights, the pressure to perform *is* real! Oh, I forgot to mention, before you took off, he pushed another button that made the weather so bad that you can barely see the runway. What will he think of next?

POWER TIP

We do everything in life for two reasons and two reasons only. One, because we want to, and two, because we have to. Take what you have to do and make it something you want to do. Then life becomes more enjoyable.

The entire two-week course is a thorough study of what makes that jet fly, everything that could possibly go wrong, and what you as the pilot must do to make it right or at least land safely under the present negative conditions.

Let's discuss a few negative situations that might happen. Unlike most small single- and twin-engine private planes, Learjets require two pilots in order to fly. Before you taxi onto the runway for takeoff, the captain, who flies from the left seat, briefs his first officer as to what actions should be taken if they lose an engine (by fire or some other malfunction). They go over what the response will be if various things happen at lower speeds and what other responses will be for emergencies at higher speeds. "Be prepared to abort or lose an engine" is always part of my preflight instructions.

Regardless of how long a pilot has been flying, all pilots are supposed to use a checklist. The pretakeoff checklist for smaller aircraft isn't quite as lengthy as a Learjet checklist, but it still applies. When I am flying a smaller, light single- or twin-engine, the first thing I say while on the runway before I add power for takeoff is, "Be prepared to abort or lose an engine!" I always say it aloud, even if I'm the only one in the plane.

Imagine the reactions I used to get from passengers who didn't know me well and were flying with me for the first time. These days I explain the be prepared concept before we board, in order to avoid the potential panic of people who don't think as I do (or I just whisper it to my copilot).

To the uninitiated, who have always been taught to use positive thinking, my words may seem quite negative. But think about it. Who would you rather fly with—a pilot who has dealt with many (simulated) engine failures or a pilot who has never practiced one? Using logic as your measuring rod, would you judge my words, "be prepared to abort or lose an engine," to be negative or realistic? Who, in their right mind, would challenge this and say it's negative?

To the uninitiated, who have always been taught to use positive thinking, my words may seem quite negative.

If it makes sense to think this way when flying an airplane with hundreds of lives on board, wouldn't it make sense to fly this way in life?

By saying out loud, "Be prepared to abort or lose an engine," I establish a mind-set that, yes, there is a degree of risk involved here, and I need to stay very focused. The method works. In fact, if there's a big enough problem, negative thinking can save your life.

Some time ago, I was on my way to the Caribbean. I rolled onto runway five and waited to receive clearance to take off. Once the air traffic controller gave me permission to take off, I acknowledged his transmission, said out loud, "Be prepared to abort or lose an engine," added power, and started my acceleration roll. Almost immediately, some of my gauges indicated that something wasn't quite right. After noticing the problem, I reacted and aborted the takeoff. And all that happened *within two seconds*!

It didn't take long for me to discover that the malfunction my gauges had indicated was nothing very serious. A very small piece of dirt was in one of my fuel injection lines. Ultimately, the problem was quite small, and airplanes have enough redundant systems that I was never in any real danger. The important thing to remember is that I didn't know the severity of my problem, and because of my negative thinking I was prepared to abort or lose an engine and was able to react rapidly. In just two seconds!

I remember flying with another pilot with whom I had never flown, and we were in his airplane. He let me take the position of Pilot In Command (PIC), so I was seated on the left. Just before takeoff, I said out loud, "Be prepared to abort or lose an engine." As the airplane began to roll down the runway, he looked over to me and said, "That's ridiculous! Nothing is going to happen."

Because of my negative thinking I was prepared to abort or lose an engine and was able to react rapidly. In just two seconds!

Talk about negative thinking . . . that's not only negative, it's *plane* stupid!

So in order to use your newfound awareness of the power of negative thoughts, you'll need to practice analyzing statements, thoughts, or ideas that appear to be negative. You'll need to be able to decide if your negative thought is a step in logical, practical planning or if it's a statement of defeat before the fact. Planning for situations where bad things might happen is smart. Assuming defeat before you start is deadly.

It's the difference between planning *on* failure or simply planning *for* problems.

A good sales professional understands that an important part of presales rehearsal is practicing overcoming objections of potential customers. It's not really practicing *for* failure. It's practicing for negative responses and determining, in advance, how to react to negative circumstances. Or better yet, it's planning how to avoid as many negative circumstances as possible before they happen. In many cases, simply planning for the negative helps you avoid problems in the first place.

So take a minute to think about negative thoughts that might be helpful to use in your own life. Are there things in your life that you believe are negative thoughts you avoid because they might generate bad outcomes or they might make you focus on the negative? They come in all shapes and sizes, and they cover personal and professional topics. If you're in sales or marketing, have you got a Plan B for your current Plan A? Do you know what you'd do if your current plan doesn't work? If you're dealing with a personal relationship (or you wish you had a personal relationship to deal with), have you avoided a confrontation or avoided asking someone out because you don't know what you'd do if you were rejected?

In many cases, simply planning for the negative helps you avoid problems in the first place.

It might help if you would put your thumb right below this paragraph, close the book, and spend a couple minutes considering negative thoughts that you've been avoiding.

Just imagine how empowered you'd be if you had a plan for dealing with all the negative things that might happen!

Now, I'm not going to get you admitting a bunch of negative thoughts and then just leave you hanging. Recognizing negative thoughts is the first part of the equation. For negative thoughts to be a powerful tool, you'll need to know as many answers as possible to the question "What would I do if this negative thing happens?" My order "Be prepared to abort or lose an engine" doesn't work if I don't know how to abort or how to deal with an engine flameout. Simply admitting potential problems isn't enough. Lots of practice and awareness of answers is equally important. Admitting that I might need to implement an emergency plan is the powerful negative thought that keeps me sharp and ready to spring into responsive action.

Simply admitting potential problems isn't enough.

I'll tell you something that I find amazing. A few paragraphs ago, when I gave the example of a sales professional practicing overcoming objections, almost everyone who has ever taken any kind of sales training was smiling to themselves because they know exactly what I'm talking about. Yet sales trainers and managers in some well-known global corporations, companies that are recognized for their sales teams, get out on the road with a fresh trainee and say, "Just imagine yourself closing the deal, and don't even think about rejection, or it'll kill you."

Wow! I guess that means it's okay to imagine you'll be rejected when you're role-playing and just overcoming objections with your sales teammates, but when you meet with actual customers in the real world, you're not supposed to entertain the thought of any kind of rejection! It's as though you're supposed to turn off that thought process just before you knock on the door or make that phone call.

I'm sure that some people reading this book feel that they completely understand the concept of using negative statements to spark the thinking process and prepare for less than perfect outcomes. In my live seminars, I read the expressions of my audiences, and I can just tell that some folks think they get it already. I talked with one of these folks at a break during a presentation once, and he said, "I understand what you mean about the power of negative thinking, but I still like to think positive about things that have neutral meaning. If you have a choice about how to look at something, as an optimist, I prefer to think positively about things."

He continued, "I'm really a 'glass-half-full' kinda guy."

I said, "I'm not." Although I do consider myself an optimist, I'm not a "glass-half-full optimist." I'm a *realist* first and an optimist second, and I'll tell you what I mean.

As I was looking for ways to get out of my depression and move on, I started getting into some of these motivational books. I wasn't impressed. In fact, it just didn't seem to be realistic or reasonable to simply avoid negative thinking. You're led to believe that if you are a positive person, the glass is half full, and if you are negative, the glass is half empty. So does that mean if I walk around with my head down and say, "The glass is half empty, the glass is half empty," that I am going to be negative? If that's true, then if I walk around in a depressed state and say, "The glass is half full, the glass is half full," I'll be a more positive person. That's ridiculous. Besides, the liquid in the glass doesn't change.

It just didn't seem to be realistic or reasonable to simply avoid negative thinking.

Let's look at this in the real world. If you give me an empty glass and I fill it up halfway, as far as I am concerned the glass is half full. If I fill the glass up with water and drink half of it, it's half empty. A fact-based interpretation doesn't need to be positive or negative; it's just a description. In his book, *How to Get Rich*, Donald Trump relates how in the early 1990s he lost focus, and when the market crashed he was in the hole to the tune of $9.2 billion. He passed a beggar on the street and realized that the beggar was worth $9.2 billion more than he was. It's a great story because it makes us laugh to think that someone who is unemployed and homeless might be worth billions more than Mr. Trump. The point to take from this is that Donald Trump looked at the negative thought as a simple statement of fact and didn't quit there. His negative thought never became a negative attitude. Certainly, you've heard of Donald Trump. Obviously, he persevered.

So practicing for possible negative circumstances helps you move forward, but in using negative thoughts, you can't always practice for *every* eventuality. Because you can't plan for everything, you'll need to at least be open to the fact that, because of all of your training and planning, you will usually be able to come up with the answers you need.

One of the leading causes of accidents in aviation today is fuel starvation. It's a typical scenario of poor fuel management. It happened to me as a young pilot. Many years ago, when I was still inexperienced, my uncle was interested in purchasing an airplane. He lived in Jamaica and wanted me to fly the airplane that he was interested in buying so he could see it. This was my longest trip ever at that time, not to mention that this was an airplane that I had never flown before. All this, coupled with flying hundreds of miles over the ocean for the first time, resulted in a real personal challenge. I left for Jamaica early one morning and finally made it at the end of the day, and it was an uneventful flight.

Because you can't plan for everything, you'll need to at least be open to the fact that, because of all of your training and planning, you will usually be able to come up with the answers you need.

My departure was planned a few days later. This leg of the trip turned out to be a bit more exciting, though. Because of my lack of experience, the long over-the-ocean flight plan, and navigating with only a compass, I was starting to run very low on fuel. The plane was so low that the needles on the fuel gauge were bouncing off the left side where the E is. That little E means a lot more at 10,000 feet over the ocean than it does behind the wheel of a car, so obviously I was scared. Everywhere I looked was ocean with no land in site.

After a few minutes of staring at the E and looking outside (it felt like an eternity), I spotted a very small island. I was able to contact an air traffic controller and made him aware of my problems and told him that I could see that there was a small runway available. He radioed back that there was no fuel on the island and I shouldn't bother.

He thought the lack of fuel on the island presented a problem for me. Not really. I basically had two choices. Land in the water, or on a runway without fuel. I may have been inexperienced, but I still had some common sense. I chose to land on a runway without available fuel. And the funny part is that the island is called Dead Man's Cay. Really!

In the end, I was able to locate a little gas on the island, and I got the plane home, but that was a lesson that I've never forgotten. Now, with much more experience under my belt, as I fly and look at my fuel gauge and the needle in the middle, is the fuel half full or half empty? Let me tell you, it's half empty, and there is nothing negative about it. Nothing!

I am amazed at how many people have such an unbalanced view about this negative, positive thinking stuff. People think, because I teach personal growth, I must be the world's greatest hypocrite when I tell them that something doesn't look as though it's going to work, or that things need to improve or heads will roll. "Oh be positive," they tell me. I *am* positive. I'm positive that I'm *prepared to abort or lose an engine.*

People think, because I teach personal growth, I must be the world's greatest hypocrite when I tell them that something doesn't look as though it's going to work.

Now that I've had to make so many aborts and lost so many engines, not in my planes, but in my professional and personal life, I am constantly preparing for them. The many deaths of loved ones I've experienced have given me a different perspective about things that happen in my day-to-day life.

In Chapter 5, we covered how trying to move on too soon frequently doesn't work. You usually need to experience the pain of negative situations before you can move past them and to the next level in your life. From that realization, you can glean another truly powerful strategy. You don't have to wait until a particular negative thing happens to experience the power that can come from that negative thought!

Back in Chapter 5 we discussed how negative life experiences can help you change and improve your attitudes and behaviors once you have reached a point where the negative experience moves from being an emotional problem to becoming simply a life experience that provides helpful information in retrospect. Even if some negative emotions remain, when you reach a point where the negative emotions are no longer overwhelming, then logical interpretation of those experiences can be a tool you can use in moving forward.

You don't have to wait until a particular negative thing happens to experience the power that can come from that negative thought!

The death of a loved one or loss of a spouse can be an overwhelmingly negative and powerful experience. As we mentioned in Chapter 5, it's okay to grieve and even cry for a while. Those things are part of the process of recognizing the loss and moving on. And consider your behavior following that kind of tragic event. You're kinder to others. You think about more deep, spiritual things. You regret things you didn't do while your loved one was alive. You think of happy times, and the thought makes you smile. All these powerful negative emotions will eventually lead to your new, enlightened perspective (if you allow it to), and hopefully you will grow as a result.

Unless you're in the middle of recovering from a recent, tragic loss, you can probably look at this clinically and agree that, after overcoming this kind of loss, you are at least somewhat more aware of the value of people and things in your life. But imagine if you had the power to have one more chance whenever something tragic in your life happened. Don't you think your attitude about that person would be more forgiving and appreciative?

You don't have to wait for something tragic, something bad, something negative to happen in order to prepare for that negative thing. In the case of being prepared to abort or lose an engine when flying, you can plan for trouble and have lifesaving measures ready to go. You can do the same in business so that you're ready for the eventualities that may present themselves. Finally, you can make exactly the same kind of preparation in life. And in any of these cases, planning for the possibility of bad or negative things yields great results, even if the bad things don't come to pass.

You can plan for trouble and have lifesaving measures ready to go.

There's a hidden treasure in this approach when it comes to interpersonal relationships. If you imagine what it would be like to lose a loved one or become tragically hurt in an accident, if you live life as though you've been given a second chance, you will squeeze every ounce of good from every minute you're alive!

I know you've heard people on the news or in a book relate a near-death experience where they almost died or were even clinically dead and then regained consciousness. Maybe you've heard of someone who experienced the sheer joy of finding a lost loved one. In both of these examples you'll hear the people involved relate how they cherish every living moment now. Their lives are richer. Their appreciation for the second chance is incredible, and their perspective of the gift of life is amazingly powerful.

I don't suggest that you meditate deeply and daily as though you *actually had* lost loved ones before they're gone. Just consider it. Imagine the emotions surrounding how you would feel. Then consider how you would behave differently when they are gone, or better yet consider how you would appreciate them so much more if you had a second chance. I assure you that you would be a far more caring, considerate, appreciative, well-rounded person if you would begin to seek all that life has to offer.

Just because people seem to be able to understand this concept as it applies to interpersonal relationships, that doesn't mean you can't do similar things in business. While using your imagination to prepare for negative things that might occur in your business, you might just invent a whole new business strategy that changes your professional life. Even if the negative thing doesn't happen, something good might come from the negative planning.

While using your imagination to prepare for negative things that might occur in your business, you might just invent a whole new business strategy that changes your professional life.

Imagine if you were in a company where you depended on one or two major clients for the majority of your income. It would be smart to plan for the possibility that you might lose that client, even if it's not likely to happen. While most people would agree that not planning for this kind of eventuality is irresponsible management, very few companies or professionals bother planning for the negative until the writing is on the wall.

In business, one of the really great things that comes from this kind of thinking is leverage. If you are a company that relies on a few major clients, those clients can use the knowledge of their importance to get you to lower your prices or do more for less. If you don't, you lose their account. If you have a plan of action ready for when they are no longer a client, *you* have the leverage. What's more, your safety net plans could just evolve into a new branch of your company.

On the individual professional level, keeping your options open can improve your attitude, your income, or both. I know a person who generally hated his job, not because it was all that difficult or paid badly. It was relatively easy and paid great. He just didn't like his job because he had been there for years. He was unfulfilled and generally bored. Friends and family all thought he was successful, and his income was quite good, but he didn't like his job, and he started looking at other positions in the classifieds. He was even considering moving (neither he nor his wife wanted to move), and he was considering a pay cut just to do something he enjoyed more.

On the individual professional level, keeping your options open can improve your attitude, your income, or both.

After a little coaching, he discovered that he enjoyed artwork, and he wanted a job that would let him do more of the kind of artwork he liked to do. Instead of taking a pay cut or an uncertain job or moving, he agreed to try simply following his art interests on weekends by participating in shows. Additionally, he agreed to stop looking for just any new job and agreed to stay in his current position until something truly great presented itself.

After changing his view that he needed to get out of his current job so he could be fulfilled and agreeing to seek fulfillment on weekends through his art, all kinds of things changed for the better. He received a few unsolicited offers for employment and decided that his present job offered the best possible balance of income, requirements, location, and so forth. He continued to be happier and more fulfilled by working on his art during evenings and weekends, and his current job got even better over time. The really great thing was that, because he was happier, he did better at work and he got raises and more interesting responsibilities and ended up liking his daily job even more.

In this case, it wasn't the job that was the problem; it was his negative attitude. And when he began to research alternatives to what he thought was the source of his negative situation, he was able to see a host of activities he could use in various ways to improve his current position. There may come a time in the near future when he gets a terrific offer and changes companies and moves, but it won't be because he's desperate for *any* change and blind to the negatives of the new opportunity. These days, he would only move on if the move was upward and positive.

As you're working on this skill, it might help if you would think about some of the negative thoughts you already use to empower yourself. In one word, I can illustrate a way that practically everyone reading this book is already using the possibility of negative outcomes to take steps that empower themselves. The word is *insurance*. People buy insurance because bad things happen. In most cases, insurance is the real-world manifestation of negative thoughts and a plan to prepare for less than perfect outcomes. It is actually a positive plan for negative possibilities.

In one word, I can illustrate a way that practically everyone reading this book is already using the possibility of negative outcomes to take steps that empower themselves. The word is **insurance.**

ATTITUDE, NOT WORDS

Consider another empowering behavior that emerges from negative thoughts. When a mother is putting her child in a car, it's considered normal for her to remind the child to put on her seat belt. If her daughter asks, "Why, Mommy?" you can already hear the response. "It's to keep you safe in case we have an accident."

We don't view the mother's statements as grossly negative or morbid, so why should we with other things?

Do you believe that the mother's recognition of the possibility of an accident is more likely to cause her to focus on the negative and cause her to have an accident? Ironically, most people would think her irresponsible if she *didn't* plan for the negative. In fact, as a society, we are so adamant about this belief that it's illegal in most states to have an unrestrained minor in a moving car.

When it comes down to handling negative thoughts and using them as empowering tools, it's important to be as clinical as possible in your view of those thoughts. I am detached from negative *emotions* when I say to my copilot, "Be prepared to abort or lose an engine." The mother explains to her child in a factual manner why the seatbelt is necessary. There's no reason to involve emotions, and it might even frighten the child unnecessarily if she did.

So how you say the negative thing is important, and it influences your ability to use the negative idea for your positive purpose. Another danger, though, is making light of the situation.

In my office, newer members of my staff will occasionally tell me to look on the bright side or be positive about some business-related situation. That's usually when they get my "Be prepared to abort" speech. People who have been on board longer always have a Plan B and long-time team members never tell me to look on the bright side of a situation. They understand that, while I may appear confrontational or I might seem to be looking at the negative side of a situation, I'm actually trying to help them search for a few positive directions they could go to improve the situation.

So how you say the negative thing is important, and it influences your ability to use the negative idea for your positive purpose.

Then, when a similar situation arises in the future and I ask employees about possible negative outcomes and what they have planned in case one or more of them happens, they don't normally tell me to be positive. They know I'm trying to help them plan. Sometimes, they even say, "I know. You want me to be prepared to abort or lose an engine."

When I hear that kind of response, I know they're on the right track. But if you push it too far in the opposite direction, you might be in as much danger as ignoring the situation entirely.

If I'm getting ready to take off and my copilot knows my stance on the "be prepared" phrase and he beats me to saying it and says it with a big smile or in a joking manner, it loses its meaning. You need to make sure your negative word strategies never become impotent through overuse or lightheartedness.

Consider how this strategy applies to business. If you're a

manager or team leader and you're thinking about applying this philosophy to your business, it's important that you recognize that this approach will yield some push-back until you take the time to explain the strategy to your team. It's important for them to all understand that the goal isn't finding fault or expecting that your employee will do something wrong. It's planning for negative possibilities so your team or your company can always be ready to move in the best possible direction.

Just because you have a plan, that doesn't mean it will be easy; it just means you have greatly improved your odds at avoiding a crash and burn.

It's time to put your new skill into practice. Start looking for negative thoughts in your personal and professional life and consider ways to (1) think more clinically about the situation in order to remove the negative emotion from the negative thought, and (2) plan for negative outcomes and practice positive responses so that you're ready for what might happen if things don't go perfectly.

SUMMARY

- Negative thinking can yield positive results.
- Planning for failure keeps us from being caught off guard.
- Too many sales professionals don't acknowledge failure as a possible outcome, so when it happens, they are devastated.
- Avoiding negative thoughts can be deadly. And, ironically, it's one of the most negative things you can do.
- Don't just acknowledge that bad things may happen; plan the best possible course of action if they do.

▌ Planning for the negative helps you—even if bad things don't happen—because you can appreciate the good outcomes that much more.

▌ Planning for negative outcomes is smart. Having a negative attitude isn't.

▌ Seat belts and insurance policies are the intelligent result of negative thoughts and planning for bad things to happen.

▌ Just because you have a plan, that doesn't mean it will be easy; it just means you have greatly improved your odds at avoiding a crash and burn.

Chapter 11

Nothing Is Good or Bad, But Thinking Makes It So!

I look back now to the tremendous losses and trials I've had in my life. The things I've lived through are a wealth of examples for my seminars and my own continued learning. One story that comes to mind occurred when I lived in a small 28-foot travel trailer. It was all I could afford at the time. I had one little bedroom. I'll never forget that bed. I'm over six feet tall, and my feet just hung off the end of the bed. And the bathroom hardly deserved the title. It wasn't roomy, nor did it even have a bath. Practically standing room only. The trailer was so small that I used to joke that I could do everything from the bathroom. Answer the phone, answer the door, and cook a meal all from the same spot. I felt that the place was constantly caving in on me. I nearly went stir crazy.

I remember this one particular night. It was about two

o'clock in the morning, and I woke up because I had to go to the bathroom. It was very dark, but at least I didn't have far to walk.

So while I was standing in my little excuse for a bathroom in the pitch black, all of a sudden I felt something soft rub against my ankle. I didn't have any pets or people living with me. It scared the living daylights out of me. I was so shocked by the furry surprise at my ankle, that I jumped up onto the bathroom sink, which barely was the size of a large frying pan.

POWER TIP

Learn to play games with your mind instead of your mind playing games with you.

As I was crouched on top of the sink, trying to control certain body functions and wishing I hadn't had so much to drink before bed, I somehow found the light switch and flipped it to reveal the source of my predicament. (By the way, my little bathroom seemed a whole lot bigger when the ordeal was over and things had to be cleaned up.) An opossum had crawled through a hole in the bottom of the trailer into the bathroom. If you know anything about opossum, they are not the fastest-moving creatures, and they can be pretty fearless. He didn't seem to want to leave. And do they look ugly when those teeth show?! So here I am on top of the bathroom sink, and I needed to shoo him out back through his little hole.

I remembered I had a broom in the tiny closet in my little bathroom. I didn't have to go far to get it. I thought all I had to do was lean over to the closet while still on the sink. You wouldn't think that would be hard in the tiny bathroom, but it was an especially complicated maneuver because of my present, urgent condition. One of my hands was already occupied. Needless to say, I finally figured out how to stay in my unique position and get a hold of the broom and escort my night visitor back out through his little hole at the bottom of the trailer.

It didn't take an opossum for me to realize that living in a 28-foot trailer was not a good and enjoyable thing to me, and it got worse before it got better. I remarried, and then my bachelor trailer was a family trailer. It was a challenge enough for one, much less adding another human. I was already frustrated and cramped, and now I had inflicted this little space on my new wife. Newlyweds are forgiving, and my wife was great about it, but my attitude in general was constantly pounded by my little trailer.

I was in need of a great escape. My wife's grandparents offered us a tremendous, timely gift. My wife wanted to visit Asia, and they offered to pay for a vacation for two! It seemed that this was exactly what we both needed. Let me pause here to emphasize the word "seemed."

We flew from Florida to California. Then, we spent hours and hours flying to Hong Kong. (I guess it was a good thing I was used to being in small spaces.) Our time there was an incredible culture shock, and to top things off, I had some pretty rough health problems at the time. Another challenge was that I was on a very strict diet. The saying in Hong Kong is that if it moves, crawls, or walks they eat it. I didn't! Then there was the incredible communication barrier.

Next, we were off to Taiwan. Wow! They literally have more motorcycles than they do people. I hadn't spent much time in big cities, as I had grown up in Jamaica, so I guess I was a little more sensitive to the pollution than the locals.

In retrospect, the trip was amazing, and experiencing the different cultures was thrilling for my wife. But because of my state of mind, the trip was awful. It seemed that wherever we went, whatever we did, my wife found the silver lining, and I got stuck with the cloud. I didn't like the trip, and I just wanted to get back. Even that was challenging and seemed to take more out of me. First we flew to Japan, then back to California, and over 24 hours later I came home to this awesome little 28-foot travel trailer. Then it was home sweet home for me!

I learned a very important lesson when I got back to my little trailer in the wee morning hours. To this day, it has changed the way I think. I knew it logically, but not emotionally. It's called perception. The length of time away and the difficulties that I experienced while gone for nearly two weeks made an indelible impression on my mind. These things that I considered negative experiences changed my perception. I remember how I felt so much relief coming home to my little 28-foot trailer.

Now, I understand that perception didn't change my circumstances but *circumstances changed my perception*. That realization helped me appreciate what I already had, no matter how little it was at the time. The next two places we moved after the trailer weren't much better, but my overseas trip helped me look at things much differently. The key is to take an experience like this and try to use the foundational principles in the other areas of life and business where they might apply.

Initially, I didn't like my little trailer, but my two-week adventure was such a negative experience for me that I loved the place. By contrast, my wife had always wanted to take a trip like that, so she really enjoyed the experience overall. We took the same trip and came back to the same trailer, but we had very different experiences. Shakespeare said it best: "Nothing is good or bad, but thinking makes it so!" What a powerful statement!

I've shared this in person with some people who don't quite understand it. They think that any bad circumstance, like taking drugs or choosing a life of crime or even murder, could very well be a good thing if you compare it to something worse. It's as if they're saying, "Look at the bright side. Things could be worse."

Both of these simplifications miss the point because they take the meaning as "things could be worse." Using that logic, people could justify criminal behavior (or any self-destructive behavior) instead of confronting current circumstances in a neutral fashion and developing a plan to forge ahead. I have found it far more powerful to use my realization so that I can say in a clinical, unemotional way, "This is how things are for now."

The statement, "Nothing is good or bad but thinking makes it so," encourages us to understand that how we view things is simply a perception. Additionally, we can come to understand that our perceptions are a choice, often not consciously planned, and they are influenced by our culture, teachers, religion, parents, and the like.

One of my favorite truths about perception is characterized in my statement, "For every positive thing you experience in your life, there are a million other people experiencing the exact same thing and hating it." It also holds true that for every *negative* thing you experience, there are a million other people experiencing the exact same thing and *loving it*.

Additionally, we can come to understand that our perceptions are a choice, often not consciously planned, and they are influenced by our culture, teachers, religion, parents, and the like.

Maybe you're thinking, *What's the harm in looking at the bright side of your present circumstances?* Probably nothing. Usually, that's an okay approach, but the problem comes when things really hit the fan. Hard. When that happens, thinking positive is a lot easier said than done. You need the more clinical approach when you can't look at the brighter side. There is a time between when something negative happens and when you can look at the bright side. We need to figure out how we can cope or make life better in those middle tough times.

For example, let's say you lose your very last $1,000 in a legitimate investment. The moment you find out that you've lost it, do you say, with a big smile, "Wow! It could be worse. At least I didn't lose $10,000"? Not if that's your last $1,000. (At least not in the real world for most people.) Maybe later you can look at the bright side of your loss, but usually not immediately while you're living through and feeling the initial negative emotions.

Now, I'm not suggesting that it's always possible but consider this. What if you could simply look at the bright side? What if you could speed up the time you experience negative emotions? Would that change your life for the better?

I recall flying to the Caribbean for a four-day getaway. The island we visited was very small, and the airport was very primitive. We had rented a pickup truck, and as I was driving the short distance to the airport, it started to rain. There were only two of us in the truck, and the back was full of luggage that belonged to half a dozen friends. I was going to pick everyone up after I had loaded the luggage onto the plane. So as it started to rain, I sped up and quickly put everything in the plane. The rain got harder and harder. The impending weather delay meant that if we didn't take off at our prescribed time, according to our filed flight plan, the plan itself plus paperwork and reporting with U.S. customs would all need to be redone. This can mean hours of delays when traveling from a third world country.

What if you could speed up the time you experience negative emotions?

As flight time approached, it kept raining hard. Now, we had to rush back to get everyone, which meant they were going to be soaking wet (they had to ride in the back of an open pickup). My soaked friends still had to clear customs before we left, and the inside of the airplane was going to be sloppy, wet, and uncomfortable for everyone.

I was really getting angry. I needed to mentally change

gears, or this emotion would take me over. As I was on my way back to get everyone, I mentally took a pit stop. Here is what came to mind: *For every positive thing you experience in your life, there are a million other people experiencing the exact same thing and hating it. For every negative thing you experience, there are a million other people experiencing the exact same thing and loving it.*

Then I thought to myself, *I'm sure if I asked them, most people would give anything to have their own private airplane, fly to a private island, and would love having it rain on them.* Given the option to stay home and watch TV versus flying myself and a few friends to a long weekend island getaway, I would take the island any time. In this case, I was able to look on the bright side of circumstances, but I didn't simply change my mind by thinking I should look on the bright side. I started by thinking about perceptions. My understanding of my bad mood being based on a perception, and my realization that nothing is good or bad but thinking makes it so, allowed me to look on the bright side. There's a slight but critical distinction that comes from the initial steps you take when analyzing a situation like this. Start by looking at your perceptions.

There's a slight but critical distinction that comes from the initial steps you take when analyzing a situation like this.

Had I stuck with my negative attitude, I would have made the trip home miserable for me and my friends. I didn't stop the pickup, hop out, jump in the puddles, and break into "Singin' in the Rain," but that's just not me. The goal here was twofold. First, I needed to stop the mental and emotional track that I was going on. Negative emotions usually breed negative emotions. (The same is true with positive emotions.) My second reason for doing this was to consciously tell myself that the experience that I am having at this moment and how I am reacting to it are the result of a perception.

This last statement bears repeating. I wanted to consciously tell myself that the experience that I was having at that moment and how I was reacting to it was *just a perception*. Again, for every negative thing you experience, there are a million people out there experiencing the same thing and loving it.

The realization that your interpretation is just a perception is something you can use as a first step toward making change. It helps you begin to regain control when you need to go from being emotionally out of control to thinking things through logically. Don't worry if you can't completely stop the negative emotion on the spot or change your perception. The more important step here is the recognition of your perception.

I recall that many years ago, when I first got into the speaking business, there was a time when things were so bad that I was minus $18,000 in my checkbook! I was constantly borrowing from Peter to pay Paul. Imagine looking into your checkbook and seeing a minus symbol beside $18,000, coupled with the thought that I had no idea how I was going to cover that amount in just a couple of days. People end up in jail for things like this, and I wasn't a criminal. I didn't want to do anything illegal, and I didn't want to go to jail! I needed money legally and in a hurry!

Don't worry if you can't completely stop the negative emotion on the spot or change your perception. The more important step here is the recognition of your perception.

I did everything I could think of with the resources I had, so later, when I finally got the balance up to *zero*, I truly felt *happy that I had no money in the bank*. What an incredibly great feeling! A zero balance in my checking account! I was thrilled. Shakespeare was right—nothing is good or bad, but thinking makes it so.

I've seen interviews with women who have been raped. Some women are devastated by the experience and have never been able to move on, while others have learned something about themselves from the tragedy, and although they would never wish for that kind of experience, they know it has made them better, stronger people.

In business and in life, we all have to take various risks in order to move ahead. Sometimes, if the risks are large and the results don't go the way we had hoped, regardless of the ultimate reason, we feel like throwing in the towel. If you've suffered some huge personal or professional loss, most people would understand your wanting to quit; they would encourage you to quit, and in fact, they'd be glad to lend you their towel. The really financially successful people like Donald Trump or Gordon "Butch" Stewart or Jack Welch have all had times in their careers when they felt devastated. Their success, their ability to overcome certain defeat, is based on their desire to keep pushing in spite of life challenges.

I have had the good fortune of seeing successful people, up close, using this strategy to their advantage, so I have understood this principle on an intellectual level for quite some time. That doesn't mean that I haven't struggled with the desire to just give up and give in. I have to use logic to help me through the really tough times. What's more, I have always had an entrepreneurial appetite, so I frequently take larger than average risks in business. That pays off sometimes, but it hurts sometimes too. I truly believe that you must fail to succeed, and I have certainly had my share of failure. People who are close to me have often commented that it's a wonder I haven't given up. With all the terrible pains and trials I've experienced, I wouldn't be able to continue at the pace I live, without the right perceptions.

I feel blessed that I have been given the insights to master the right perceptions, and one of the reasons for this book is that I want to share that mastery with everyone I can. If I let my past bad experiences be the sole basis for defining who I am or what my life is supposed to be like, I would begin to feel not only like a total failure but even jinxed.

I have had the good fortune of seeing successful people, up close, using this strategy to their advantage so I have understood this principle on an intellectual level for quite some time.

Now I mentioned something earlier that I feel deserves a bit more explanation. I believe that you must fail to succeed. I relate this idea to Babe Ruth. Most of us have heard the story. Babe Ruth was famous for setting home run records but most of us have heard by now that he was also the strikeout king.

It's not really all that shocking if you think about it. We all have to step up to the plate. If we are willing to consistently do that, our actions will lead to results. Even a blind squirrel finds a nut once in awhile!

We can use the realization that perceptions aren't absolutes and the concept that we need to keep trying until we're able to achieve the results we're seeking, in order to make quantum leaps in how we internalize things. That will give us much more control over our lives and our happiness.

I have a book in the back seat of one of my airplanes, and I forget it's there from time to time. I am occasionally reminded by passengers of my book when they sift through the pouch of one of the back seat pockets and discover it. Usually people laugh. Some laugh nervously. My book is called *Why Planes Crash*. Now, by no means is it negative to read about planes crashing. If I can possibly learn from others' mistakes instead of my own, I'm ahead of the game. The book is full of stupid, and not so stupid, things pilots have done. I have a subscription that comes to me monthly, and it's all about accidents. It has changed the way I fly. To this day, I'll do specific things, and I realize that I'm only doing or thinking about them because I read a story about a specific accident. I believe I'm a much safer pilot than if I had just studied what the FAA requires.

When I started flying Learjets, I started a log of every little thing that I did wrong (nothing dramatic or life threatening), where it happened, the situation, and what needed to be done to correct it. I can read through that log right now, and it reminds me of every emotion and detail. This log is simply designed to make me a better pilot.

I've already shared with you the challenges of instrument flying. I have created a binder on any observation, mistakes, or improvements that I could make, and from time to time, before I go flying I will brush up on it. If I'm on a long flight, I'll take it with me to read. (Yes, I read while I'm flying. That's what the autopilot can do for you.) To many people, accident reports recount a tragedy (a bad thing), and to me I am using the exact same information to be a better pilot (a good thing). Nothing is good or bad, but thinking makes it so.

To many people, accident reports recount a tragedy (a bad thing), and to me I am using the exact same information to be a better pilot (a good thing).

Recall earlier that I shared with you how important it is to try to make yourself consciously understand that your experiences and how you react to them are often based on your perceptions. We should continually look for ways to master these perceptions. Let's stay focused on that.

One of my tools is something I call Attitude Adjusting Statements. There are certain phrases that the moment you say them, you automatically program yourself for negativity. See if you can finish the sentences with me before I do.

- If it ain't one thing, it's _____.
- When it rains it _____!

Now, when have you *ever* seen someone who is making tons of money, with a great life, come up to you and say, "If it ain't one thing, it's another?" You'd never hear them say, "When it rains it pours!" No way! It doesn't happen. Would you also agree that the moment we make one of these statements, whatever happens next that is just slightly negative, is viewed as being even more negative than it deserves? Using these negative statements sets us up for a negative view. We are going to make things worse than they really are.

It's a perfect way to set yourself up for a negative day. But really it's just a perception, and if you don't accept the negative interpretation, it can't keep bringing you down.

Using these negative statements sets us up for a negative view. We are going to make things worse than they really are.

I feel compelled to make a brief legal disclaimer about my supposition that "if it ain't one thing it's another" is always untrue. The time when it *is* true is when you own a boat or a plane. When it comes to repairs, the hard, cold fact is that if it's not one thing it's another! But for life, stay away from these statements.

The point here, especially if you have a tendency to say any of these things, is to not buy into these statements. If you start saying one of them, bite your tongue. This will be another way of telling yourself that you are aware that you were just about to buy into this perception.

It's possible that once you understand the perception thing, you will want to share it with the world. Maybe you can help some friends or family, but be careful how and where you decide to help someone change attitude adjusting statements.

Let's say one day you are in the grocery store and as you

are in line, there is a lady with three young kids at the register next to you. You can overhear everything she's saying. She has a two-year-old on her hip with food hanging out of its mouth, the other two toddlers are tugging at her and wanting to buy candy that they see in the checkout displays, and as she tries to hush them, she drops some of her groceries as she tries to put them on the conveyor belt. Then you hear those words, "When it rains it pours."

Now imagine leaning over to her while she struggles to pick up the celery from the floor, and then you gently whisper, "You know, that is simply a perception." You had better duck, because you're about to be slapped or have one of those kids thrown at you.

You just can't say that. The timing isn't right. So, if someone said one of these negative statements to you, even in jest, how do you respond to a situation like this and not sound like a know-it-all? There's actually something you can say back that is both true and might just help other people see that their statements are just perceptions. This statement and others like it will do two things for you. One, it will show that you are listening and sympathetic to the other person's problems. Second, it will consciously keep you in tune with the fact that you are observing a situation that is fueled by a possible wrong perception. I'll tell you what the statement is, but first let me tell you how I used it in real life.

I used it to help a very good friend at one of the lowest points in her life. Clem had been married to her husband Bill for nearly 50 years. I received a call early one Saturday morning with the terrible news. Bill had suddenly died. I flew to Bill's funeral to show my support and to be with the family.

The next day I called Clem to see how she was holding up. Her situation had gotten worse. Bill's close friend, whom I knew and had seen at the funeral, died from a sudden heart attack the very next day. Poor Clem. She just buried her husband, and now she's on the way to New York a few days later to bury one of her husband's best friends. At this point, Clem and her friends were feeling a bit paranoid. The thought crossed their minds, *What's going to happen next?* From the time of Bill's death, I committed to myself that I would spend the next year helping Clem to get through all this, over the phone, or occasionally stopping by when I was flying through her state. Whatever it took.

Before she flew to New York for the second funeral we had a very long phone conversation with her and one of her friends. The situation that needed to be addressed immediately was how to assist her in keeping her sanity when so many negative things were happening to her at once. She was scared and emotionally drained. If she continued, she could go deeper into a depressed state, if not a suicidal one.

In our conversations, I had suggested that by this time that many of her very close friends were likely saying to her and each other, "It feels as though our world is caving in." She acknowledged that it was already happening.

Because of what I know about how people program themselves, I knew that my friend was going to be confronted with the opportunity to program herself in the near future. How Clem responded to the caving in statement would program her for success or failure. If she said, "I know. It does feel like our world is caving in on us," she would only make it harder for herself. This kind of response indicates that she has bought into the perception that her world is caving in and more bad things are sure to follow.

Here is what I told Clem and her friend to say when people say things like this. Repeat the statement and add one word. It's the same kind of thing you could say to the lady in the grocery line. Clem's response should be, "It certainly *seems* like things are caving in." In talking with the lady in the grocery store I would say, "It certainly seems that way." The moment either woman decides not to agree with the negative statements outright, even if she acknowledges that things may *seem* negative, she has now attempted to put a stop to allowing her emotions to get worse.

At this point, we weren't trying to make her feel happy. It wasn't time for her to make her lemonade yet. It wasn't time to look on the bright side. She had just lost someone who had shared everything with her for nearly 50 years. My goal for her was to help her get through her tragedy and not get any worse. I knew if she could manage her perceptions of these life-changing events, she could make it through.

I knew if she could manage her perceptions of these life-changing events, she could make it through.

There's another powerful benefit to her new response and perhaps it's the most important. It is the fact that it takes conscious effort for her to make the choice to respond this way. This choice, deciding not to buy into the negative perception, keeps her headed in the right direction, and it's incredibly empowering.

SUMMARY

▍ Perception isn't reality.

▍ One of the first steps toward changing your perception is recognizing that how you feel about something is just a perception, and perceptions can be changed.

▍ For every positive thing you experience in your life, there are a million other people experiencing the exact same thing and hating it.

▌ It also holds true that for every *negative* thing you experience, there are a million other people experiencing the exact same thing and *loving it*.

▌ If your perception yields the wrong results, change your perception.

▌ Choosing to change your perception gives you back a degree of control over your circumstances and is quite empowering.

Chapter 12

Positive Thinking Is a Lie, But It's a Start

You already know why I think positive thinking is a hoax. It's not the answer, and when it's presented as a cure, in and of itself, it can even be detrimental. Obviously, though, there is something to positive thinking. It's just that there are nuances you must understand about how and when it can be used effectively. Remember that I told you it takes practice to see what at first appears to be splitting hairs? The hair that we're splitting here is that positive thinking is a hoax, but there are ways you can use positive thinking as a tool.

Ultimately, the problem with positive thinking is that it is usually presented as a way of overcoming a challenge or a way to reach a goal. It is neither. You can use positive thinking in two very specific ways and get desired results. One way is using positive thinking as it comes naturally, and the other way is as a method of lying about how you feel in order to get started in an appropriate direction. Ironically, this second method seems to imply that I'm suggesting exactly what positive thinking/positive affirmation schools of thought teach, and I've already told you that this kind of positive thinking is a hoax. So let's break it down further.

The way we learn to use positive thinking is a natural result of the way the reactionary part of our brain is wired by our creator. Although this is mostly a good thing, there are times when some aspects of natural positive thinking can be misinterpreted, so that's when we need to use another gift from our creator, our intellect, to modify our perception of the times when positive thinking doesn't work. Also, we need to be intellectually aware that there are times when trying to think positive isn't appropriate at all. First let's consider how positive thinking works naturally.

We need to be intellectually aware that there are times when trying to think positive isn't appropriate at all.

Let's say we are working on losing weight. We've made adjustments to our diet and are starting some type of exercise program. A week or so later, we get on the scale and see some improvement. We've lost some weight, and we feel good about it. Then after we get off the scale, we say something like, "I know I can do this!" In this case, the statement, "I know I can do this," is positive thinking, and it's backed up by hard evidence. The key here is that, because we are certain that we are making progress and the scale confirms it, when we make positive statements, we believe they are true, and we can lose more weight. This is actually the beginning of thoroughly developed positive attitude that can help drive almost anyone to higher personal and professional levels of achievement.

POWER TIP

Pretend you are hungry even when you are full.

We try to stick to the diet, but in spite of our best intentions, the next week things don't seem to go as well. Our routine got out of whack, and our diet has really been a mess. We get back on the scale, and the weight we lost last week has come back and then some. Now we are feeling very discouraged. Because we're trying to be positive and use positive thinking and affirmations, we say, "I know that I can do this." This time, there's a difference compared to the first time we made the exact same positive statement. That little place inside us where we hid our negative thoughts comes to the surface, and we have an internal conflict. Our doubt conflicts with the positive affirmation.

We are saying something that is the opposite of how we feel. We really feel discouraged due to our results, and the positive affirmation just makes us feel that we are lying. And truthfully, that is exactly what we are doing.

The problem gets worse. When we try to use positive affirmations and we simultaneously feel bad, we begin to reason that positive thinking isn't working. If we simply use positive affirmations regardless of our conflict with our beliefs and our results, we're destined to at least think that positive thinking doesn't work, but more likely we lay the blame on ourselves. It starts a big, negative snowball rolling down the hill, and every time we use more positive affirmations, we keep feeling worse. We've got to stop that snowball from rolling before we're completely out of control.

When we try to use positive affirmations and we simultaneously feel bad, we begin to reason that positive thinking isn't working.

Remember I told you there was a natural way positive thinking works? That's because whenever we use positive statements or affirmations and the evidence and our feelings agree with the statements, positive thinking works. That is the natural way.

Pop psychology experts skate by when they suggest using

positive thinking and further suggest that you just suppress or ignore negative feelings until you reach a goal. If we have a goal to reach or challenge to overcome, positive thinking and affirmations *might* work if we can suppress our doubt and keep chanting our affirmations louder and longer. Unfortunately, this will work only to a limited degree, because it's not intellectually honest and the really big goals and challenges have correspondingly large doubts associated with them. I guess these people think positive thinking can work or help someone to power through a difficult time because they haven't lived through the really bad times with really powerful doubts. I have. That's why I'm sure positive thinking doesn't work all the time.

To get to the next level and craft positive thinking into a useful tool that we can use when it fits our circumstances, we need to use our intellect. We also need to use our intellect to avoid using positive thinking when we know it won't work.

Emotions are often unconscious and largely instinctual. They serve animals well, and in many cases, emotions serve humans. With animals, their primitive emotions of fear keep them alive. Their emotions of family keep their pack or family group together and help them to protect one another. With humans, our reactionary emotions serve us well in early life, and our fear emotions might save us from stepping into traffic or standing too close to the edge of a canyon cliff.

We also need to use our intellect to avoid using positive thinking when we know it won't work.

Because we as humans are intellectually gifted, we understand that sometimes animals are served poorly by their instinct and primitive emotions. Consider a housecat who lives the good life. He's indoors 24/7, never has to worry about hunting the next meal, has full run of the house, and goes wherever he wants whenever he wants. His (human) family is amazingly affectionate and no harm has ever come to this precious ball of fluff. When the family goes on vacation for a couple of weeks and wants to take fuzz ball along, he completely panics. The fear of riding in a car overrides everything the cat knows about his human friends, and his fear may be so strong it causes him to hurt himself in a vain attempt to get out of his travel carrier.

We humans can see that there's no reason for the cat to be afraid and if he would just calm down, he'd be just fine. And we humans also understand that if we control our emotions when they are in conflict with intellectual evidence, we will benefit.

POWER TIP

Passion is great. But without fuel, it quickly dies.

It's likely that you know someone who seems to be in total control of his emotions. Most people admire this kind of control. We say that a person is together, and society generally looks up to this kind of in-control personality. Unless that person has a psychological disorder, he or she has emotions, it's just that the emotions don't ever seem to control behavior or decision making, and that's what we admire.

Although it's a worthwhile pursuit to control your emotions and be this kind of together person, there's another, richer level of emotional control we can reach if we use our intellect to direct our emotions and use their power, channeled in the right direction, to help us reach a goal or overcome a challenge. People who can use positive and negative emotions to their own benefit are even more together than someone who seems to simply dismiss their emotions in favor of the purely intellectual "Vulcan" approach.

Although it's a worthwhile pursuit to control your emotions and be this kind of together person, there's another, richer level of emotional control.

Children are not fully developed emotionally until they become adults; the following information applies to adults with no clinical mental disorders. *Group A:* This is a small portion of the population that is driven almost entirely emotionally with very little intellectual influence over their behavior. *Group B:* This is the largest group of the population, in which decisions are emotionally driven with some intellectual influences. This group has some intellectual control over things that are not emotionally charged issues for them, but powerful issues are almost always decided by the more primitive emotional drive rather than by intellect. *Group C:* Smaller than Group B, this group has emotions but has learned to control them in favor of intellectual considerations. These individuals are often admired by others as being well-adjusted, thoughtful, together people. *Group D:* Generally the smallest group, these people understand the power of emotions and the power of controlling them. They have decided to move beyond Group C, and they have chosen to channel powerful emotions in order to achieve goals and overcome obstacles that simple, intellectual consideration alone couldn't master.

One of my millionaire mentors shared a strategy with me once that is a perfect example of how he went from experiencing a negative emotion, to taking the sting out of the negative experience, and then channeling this negative emotion into a positive force that drives him to even greater success. He shared the philosophy that frustration equals success.

He explains it this way: "When I first start out on a project, if it's something new and innovative, I'll have to learn how to do various aspects of this project along the way. If it was easy someone would have already figured it out. I used to get caught up in the frustrations along the way, and those negative emotions would cause me to make bad decisions, look for an easy way out, or even cut and run. Eventually, though, by pushing through the frustrations, I reached a really big goal and set a whole new standard for the way my industry does business."

He shared the philosophy that frustration equals success.

He continued, "I realized that the frustrations were simply a part of getting to my goal, and those same frustrations kept my competition from reaching that same goal before me. Now when I embark on some new, challenging undertaking, I don't just expect frustrations, I welcome them. It took a long time for me to get to this point, but now when frustrating things happen, it makes me smile. They push me to overcome them, and I use frustrations as a motivating emotional push to reach my goals."

"This doesn't mean that I never get frustrated. It just means that most things that used to frustrate me now inspire me. One more thing . . . As I've overcome challenges and reached higher and higher goals in my business, the number and type of frustrations that arise often grows. I still have to keep reminding myself that frustration equals success so I don't get caught up in the new frustrations."

As I've overcome challenges and reached higher and higher goals in my business, the number and type of frustrations that arise often grows.

This person has truly mastered his emotions because he doesn't simply suppress his frustrations to achieve his goals as a together person would. He uses his intellect to channel his frustrations and negative emotions, and converts this negative energy into positive emotions that drive him to the realizations of his goals.

When it comes to using positive thinking as an effective tool, you will benefit most if you can look at optimism and positive thinking from an intellectual perspective.

Right up front, let's admit that positive thinking, and emotional control in general, may be beyond your intellectual grasp if you're experiencing the very recent loss of a loved one, a major business failure, a relationship loss, or deep, clinical depression. In the case of clinical depression or other psychological disorders, there is frequently no self-treatment that can match the intervention of an expert. In these cases, it's best to seek professional help. In the case of a devastating business loss, the loss of a loved one, or other traumatic life experience, you may need to let a little time pass before you try to tackle channeling your emotions and using positive thinking as a tool. As I mentioned elsewhere in this book, if you're rebounding from a major loss, you might not be able to look at the bright side of things right away. Sometimes, all you can do is remind yourself that however bad things *seem*, that isn't how they truly are.

In order to be able to look at positive thinking intellectually, so that you can master it and use it as a tool you need to understand the internal conflict that arises whenever you feel that you're lying to yourself.

The first problem that you need to fix is a feeling. When we first lost the weight, we truly felt that we could to it. The scale confirmed the positive feelings by the results it displayed. So when we said the positive affirmations while we felt positive, we concluded that everything was okay. By contrast, when we try to say them again while feeling discouraged or negative, we feel as if we are lying.

In order to be able to look at positive thinking intellectually, so that you can master it and use it as a tool you need to understand the internal conflict that arises whenever you feel that you're lying to yourself.

We feel as though we're lying because what we say is the opposite of how we feel. We've been taught from childhood that lying is not good, so what do we do? Most people resolve the conflict by quitting the lie. In other words, we stop saying something that's the opposite of how we feel, but now we end up going back to being discouraged. We reward the negative feeling. Even if you've made progress toward a goal, frequently this is where the progress stops. If you make the intellectual decision to persevere, it usually helps if you can understand that whenever your feelings conflict with positive thinking, then positive thinking is lying. But it is a start. Consider the alternative. Feel bad and say something negative to go along with the feeling. We don't want negative feelings or negative results, so that option is out.

Start by remembering that the lie we're using as our starting point isn't intended as deceit, and the goal is a good one, so in order to use positive thinking as a starting point, you have to believe that *this* lie is a helpful lie. That may be tough. From the moment we were born, we have been programmed to be a slave to our feelings because they've served us well for so long. We feel hungry, so we cry. We get fed. We feel as though we want to be picked up, we cry. We get picked up. We feel uncomfortable because we have a soiled diaper, so we cry. The diaper gets changed. As we get older, other things happen to us that cause us to feel sad, so we act sad. When we feel happy, we act happy. Things like this start creating a pattern, and it's natural to become a slave to our feelings. We slowly begin to lose emotional control, and we get blown about like paper in the wind. Whenever people lack emotional control, they tend to feel first and think last. If we can *think first* and *feel last*, we can channel our emotions and use them as tools. Simply stopping to consider an emotion intellectually creates a moment for you to make choices. These choices can break the bonds that keep many people as slaves to their feelings.

*Whenever people lack emotional control, they tend to feel first and think last. If we can **think first** and **feel last**, we can channel our emotions and use them as tools.*

When people are unable to mentally stop and make these emotional choices, they become easily programmed by external stimuli. There should really come a point in everyone's life when he should say, "Stop. Let me mentally chew on this. I can choose to allow this situation or circumstance to influence me emotionally or not." As you read this, I challenge you to make that choice right now. Stop reading for a moment, and make a conscious decision to stop before letting any emotion direct your actions.

It may take a bit of practice, but you are going to have to remember that you need to be aware of your feelings as often and as completely as possible. Next, you need to determine if your feelings are in harmony with our goals. If they are, great! Reward your feelings, and go along with them. If your feelings aren't in harmony with your goals, it's time to start lying. Use your intellectual understanding that your feelings are wrong.

So the natural way of using positive thinking is when we feel positive, we say positive things, and this energizes us to keep going. The wrong way to use positive thinking is to force it on ourselves when we don't feel it, and then, when we feel that positive thinking is wrong, to simply try to suppress our doubt and sweep the feelings of conflict under the rug. The *right* way to use positive thinking is the intellectual way where we don't just control our emotions, we master them and channel our feelings and emotions to get us to the results we need.

*The **right** way to use positive thinking is the intellectual way.*

Once you understand the power of mastering and channeling emotions, the big question still remaining for most people is how? Generally, you need to mentally stop any time you feel that an emotion is starting to control your actions, and you must decide whether that feeling is in harmony with your goals. Most people don't need help controlling simple situations that don't stir deep emotional reaction. The challenge is controlling powerful emotions tied to important business and life goals. I've developed a few techniques for these more challenging situations.

TECHNIQUE ONE

This technique is designed to help you master the ability to move on following a painful personal experience. Think about a time in your past that was really hard for you, either personally or professionally. Inevitably, there were people in your life who meant well but said the wrong thing. After a while, after we recovered a bit from the initial trauma, we realized that what our friends said that seemed like the wrong thing was really the right thing. They just said it at the wrong time.

Remember that I told you about my experience that my wife told me our baby wasn't mine. One of my friends said, "At least you don't have to pay child support for the next 18 years." Talk about insensitive!

But wait a minute. Maybe in one, two, or ten years I might appreciate that point. Yeah, at least I don't have to pay child support for the next 18 years. These days, that statement is even kind of funny to me.

Studies have been done with patients in mental institutions who were diagnosed with mental disorders. They were asked to answer a number of questions, and their answers reflected their diagnosis. When those same subjects were asked to answer those same questions "like a normal, sane person would," their scores were greatly improved. They knew how normal people should respond, and that helped them improve their responses.

So begin with the end in mind. If we could look now with the end in mind and ask ourselves, "Five or ten years from now if I had overcome this business or personal challenge, what would I be saying?" Once you figure out what it is that you would be saying, try to adopt that attitude as soon as you can. It's not uncommon to hear someone say, "One day, you'll look back and laugh at all this." The goal here is to make that one day come as soon as possible. The quicker you can make that day come, the quicker you'll let yourself laugh. *Time doesn't heal all wounds, you do.*

Begin with the end in mind.

Take a minute and write down a joke or some positive thing you would say if you could put emotions and sensitivity aside. You really have to detach yourself emotionally to be able to do this. The more recent the situation, the more you are going to feel that you are lying, but remember that the lie is okay because your goal is to overcome the negative emotion and control it. The negative emotion isn't in harmony with your goals. Start with the end in mind, and imagine a future time when positive thinking will come naturally. The goal is to get your thoughts to match your feelings. You'll need to use your intellect to imagine your future positive thinking and to keep thinking in that direction until your thoughts and feelings match. Use your thoughts to guide your feelings.

TECHNIQUE TWO

I use this technique to reinforce the idea that I have the ability to control my emotions most of the time. It may be natural to let feelings and emotions flow freely when something good happens and you're excited about it. Often, I will take a moment in the middle of some good situation and consciously tone down my excitement, even if it's just for a second or two.

The lesson I'm teaching myself and constantly reinforcing is that I have the intellectual ability to control my positive and negative emotions, and I reinforce this with myself regularly. If you get in the habit of doing this when you don't have to, it helps you master those times when you *need* to control and channel your feelings and emotions.

Often, I will take a moment in the middle of some good situation and consciously tone down my excitement, even if it's just for a second or two.

The more we try to move on in life, sales, or our profession and push forward, the more we are likely to experience internal emotional resistance. To keep growing and improving, your challenges will change and new frustrations will arise. To stay on top of things, you'll have to keep lying and channeling your emotions, ignoring your feelings, and moving forward, based on your intellectual decisions until your feelings fall in line with your intellect and beliefs.

If you can master this you'll be one of those together people who always seem to keep moving ahead.

SUMMARY

- The problem with positive thinking is that it is usually presented as a way of overcoming a challenge or a way to reach a goal. It is neither.

- Natural positive thinking can reinforce appropriate behavior, and that's good.

- Forcing positive thoughts or using affirmations will almost never work, until you understand the underlying reason why you don't feel naturally positive about the particular circumstance.

▌ It's a worthwhile pursuit to control your emotions and be a together person, yet there's another richer level of emotional control we can reach if we use our intellect to direct our emotions and use the power of emotions, channeled in the right direction, to help us reach a goal or overcome a challenge.

▌ Understanding and mastering your emotions can help you logically change negative feelings into positive ones. Technically this is forcing positive thinking, but it's not something you achieve by ignoring the initial negative feelings and simply powering through.

▌ In order to be able to look at positive thinking intellectually, so that you can master it and use it as a tool, you need to understand the internal conflict that arises whenever you feel that you're lying to yourself.

▌ *First:* You need to be aware of your feelings as often and as completely as possible.

▌ *Next:* You need to determine if your feelings are in harmony with your goals. If they are, great!

▌ *Finally:* If your feelings *aren't* in harmony with your goals, it's time to use your intellectual understanding that your feelings are wrong and work to change them.

▌ You can begin with the end in mind and imagine how you would feel if you had lived past the pain of a negative event.

▌ Briefly stop and control your positive emotions in a good situation, as a means of reminding yourself that you are always in control of your emotions if you choose to be.

▌ To stay on top of things, you'll have to keep channeling your emotions, ignoring your feelings, and moving forward based on your intellectual decisions until your feelings fall in line with your intellect and beliefs.

Chapter 13

Rewiring Your Brain— Going beyond Positive Thinking: The Four-Step Process

AN AMAZING POWER TOOL FOR REWIRING YOUR BRAIN: THE FOUR-STEP PROCESS

This book is loaded with little things you can do to improve various situations in your life, but what you're about to learn is what has made me famous. It's the single best way to rewire your brain to achieve the results you want, and I call it the Four-Step Process. If you can truly master all the aspects of the Four-Step Process, and understand why each is important, you're on the road to being able to overcome practically any problem or challenge in your life. You'll rewire your brain.

It has been my experience that the Four-Step Process will only truly work for you if you understand the psychology of the process and how the steps relate to one another. And it's not necessarily a linear process. You may need to jump around between the steps, and if you don't understand the process completely, managing your use of the four steps will be impossible.

The Four-Step Process is where everything I've told you thus far about success, failure, psychology, human behavior, and so-called solutions will all come together. You'll need to keep an open mind in order for all of the steps to make sense. Here's what I mean. In earlier chapters, I've told you how positive thinking is a hoax. You're about to learn that it's not so much positive thinking itself that's the hoax, it's the way it is presented; namely, as a solution in and of itself. In fact, one of the steps of the Four-Step Process is actually a form of positive thinking but without the other three steps and their relationship to the positive thinking process, it would be worthless.

WHERE TO START WITH THE FOUR-STEP PROCESS

Because this process is intended to change any negative behavior or negative thought process, it's time to tackle your own biggest problem. Grab a legal pad and something to write with, and go to the kitchen table.

This process is intended to change any negative behavior or negative thought process.

Whenever I do personal consulting, I start by having my client prepare for our consultation by getting four pieces of legal paper and something to write with. On the top right corner of the first page, we'll put the number 1 there and circle it, and we'll do the same for pages 2, 3, and 4. Go ahead and do this yourself now. Put all four sheets side-by-side and number the pages.

JUST TO KEEP THINGS STRAIGHT

The Four-Step Process is a collection of exercises that all interrelate. The way they are presented is by using four sheets of paper to keep things straight, but at various places along the way, we may refer to your page 3 while working on Step Four. As we proceed, it may seem as though we're jumping around from one of your pages to another, but as long as you don't equate each step of the Four-Step Process with the corresponding numbered page, you'll be fine.

POWER TIP

Our ability to handle or not handle rejection is often related to our perception of how others may view us.

THE POWER OF FEAR CAN
BE OVERWHELMING

I use stories and examples throughout my seminars and in this book, and they are intended to illustrate my point in a more powerful way than a clinical explanation ever could. Keep in mind as you read the following example that helping to coach someone through a phobia is one of the most dramatic ways I can demonstrate the power of the Four-Step Process, and that's why I use it. I am not a doctor and, even though I help people overcome phobias, that's not the point. I simply want to illustrate, as dramatically as possible, that applying the Four-Step Process is incredibly powerful. The phobia illustration is ideal to help an audience understand my message.

One more thing, curing a severe phobia usually requires a coach who is deeply rooted in the Four-Step Process and emotionally detached from the phobia itself. The reason a phobia is so powerful is that it's rooted in the deepest emotions and beliefs of a person. A phobic personality doesn't have the emotional control to move between the four steps as we all need to do in order to make a change. The Four-Step Process is powerful, but so are phobias, and although you will be able to make powerful, sweeping changes in your life, in many cases only a trained coach can help a severe phobic personality overcome a phobia through this process.

At my live seminars, I do a demonstration using the Four-Step Process in which I take someone from the audience who is very phobic and, in a matter of minutes, completely reverse the phobia. I look for the worst cases in the audience and I don't care how many years they have been plagued with their phobia. This process enables me to do in less than an hour what many therapists are unable to accomplish in a year of using traditional therapies.

The Four-Step Process is powerful, but so are phobias, and although you will be able to make powerful, sweeping changes in your life, in many cases only a trained coach can help a severe phobic personality overcome a phobia through this process.

For Step One to work we need to determine why the behavior must be changed. I can promise you this is not as easy as it may seem. After identifying something you want to change, you need to ask yourself, "Why must I change this behavior?"

YOUR STEP ONE IS YOUR PAGE 1

Step One in our process is to write down, "Why must I change this behavior?" Write this at the top of page 1. (Page 1 represents Step One and so on.) Once you write that question, you next need to answer the question, but don't write down your answer yet, because I want you to write the correct answer, not just any answer. I'll tell you when it's time to write your answers.

The following four pages illustrate what your Process Pages should contain. You can recreate them or write right in this book.

(1)

The behavior I want to change (or challenge I want to overcome) is:

_____

_____

Why must I change this behavior?

_____

_____

_____

②

Empowering Beliefs or Thoughts (the opposite of page 4)

For every thought we act on we get a result

_____

_____

_____

_____

Remember, Feelings Change Last

③

New Positive Feelings and Experiences

_____

_____

_____

_____

_____

④

Limited Beliefs or Thoughts

_____

_____

_____

_____

Most people have what they believe are great answers for this question but unless they are truly powerful reasons, your commitment to change will fall far short.

Allow me to illustrate it this way. Let's say that I am in front of an audience with 1,000 people who smoke cigarettes. I ask the audience, "How many of you would like to quit smoking?" I think you'll agree that a large majority of that audience will raise their hands. At this point, I ask the audience to write down the reasons why they want to change this habit or behavior. I assume that all those who said they want to quit will also have great reasons why they should. It has been my experience that many people are into personal growth but lack a complete understanding of how the mind really works. They simply tell people that you must have a why. You've probably even heard someone ask, "What's your why?"

It's likely that many audience members will have dozens of reasons why they want to change. Great, but that's not enough. You must not assume that if people have one or several reasons why they want to change, they will, in fact, change. It takes more than that, but it is at least a start.

You must not assume that if people have one or several reasons why they want to change, they will, in fact, change.

So let's take my analogy even further. Out of this audience of a thousand people, I decide to pick two people and bring them on stage. I ask both people to show me their list. The first person has only one reason on the page about why he wants to quit. The second person has forty.

So who would you think has the greatest odds of succeeding? Be careful how you answer this question. It seems like common sense that it would obviously be the person with the most answers. Interestingly enough, though, the number of reasons you have on your list on your page 1 has nothing to do with your potential success or failure. So then, which one of these people will have the greatest odds of changing? The answer is simply the person who has placed the greatest value on his reason, whether it is one reason or one hundred. So a person who has only written down a single reason for changing, can outperform another who has hundreds of reasons. Why? Because the person with one reason has placed more importance or value on that one reason than all the combined reasons of the other person.

A person who has only written down a single reason for changing, can outperform another who has hundreds of reasons.

When I start a consultation and my client has completed page 1, as I point to the reasons he has written down, I tell him that as far as I am concerned, what he has written down are just words on a piece of paper and words are cheap! As we continue with the Four-Step Process, we will start to see if they are simply words on a piece of paper, or if the client is truly able to use this page as leverage to make changes in his life. This becomes very obvious as my consultation progresses, and I will explain how you can make this determination as we continue.

It's time to write down your page 1 answers (what I want to change and why). Take a few minutes, and do that now. As you move on to Step Two keep page 1 handy because we will be regularly referring back to Step One throughout the Four-Step Process. If you haven't already, take a minute to identify a result in your life you don't like and the behavior(s) that leads to the poor results.

STEP TWO IS PAGE 4

Now it's time to go to Step Two. Take out the piece of paper you numbered 4. That's right, our second step is page 4 not page 2. Because we have already discussed the importance of acknowledging the need to change, in Step Two we need to figure out how we can identify the negative trash that's in our mind and put all that information on paper so we can effectively try to change it.

Defining your limiting beliefs is critical in order to overcome them. It's important to understand that for every thought we act on we get a result. Almost all results we get in life, (financial, physical, mental, and emotional) stem from our thought process. If we have a negative thought, and reward it, we'll usually get a negative result. The reverse is just as true. For every positive thought we act on, we get a positive result. The goal for your page 4 is to identify all the negative thoughts that creep up. It's the negative thoughts that we reward that create the negative results. Before we can make a change from negative to positive it's important to identify what our negative thoughts are telling us and the results that they cause. Your page 4 is the stuff that rents space in your head and needs to be evicted.

It's the negative thoughts that we reward that create the negative results.

Page 4 needs a heading. Write "Limited Beliefs or Thoughts." It's time to figure out what's going on in your mind and put it on paper.

As I mention in my live seminars, I use this Four-Step Process to help rid a phobia. Because in any audience there is usually someone with a terrible phobia of spiders, I frequently use this phobia in my demonstrations. Let me interject once again that people with a very deep-seated phobia will usually not be able to do this entirely on their own. The main reason is because phobic people specifically lack adequate emotional control of their phobic responses because they are unable to think rationally.

To expose the thought process or mind-set that's causing the phobia, I ask a series of questions. And before I even ask any questions, I ask the person to try to think the answer through logically and not emotionally. I might then ask, "If I were to bring several spiders in front of you right now, what would go through your mind?" Phobias are so powerful that I have to caution them in advance to think logically, because the true phobic mind can't handle the idea of just thinking about a spider near them, much less several.

But if I can get them to at least momentarily dwell on the possibility of being exposed to some spiders, I will get some answers. Again, the question is "If I were to bring several spiders in front of you right now what would go through your mind?"

I've done this so many times that I know what the answers will usually be. Typical answers include "They are going to crawl on me" or "I'll have to scream and run away" or "They're going to attack me!"

If they hesitate at all before answering, I let them know that I don't care how silly, stupid, negative, or irrational the answer is. We need to know whatever the answer truly is so that we have something to work with. I don't care how negative it sounds. Remember, it's the negative thought which they are rewarding that causes the negative result. This person's page 4 will contain all of their limiting beliefs and negative thoughts that keep the person from being able to hold, touch, or even look at a spider.

What's truly amazing here is that if you are not bothered by spiders but you somehow started to believe the thoughts "They are going to crawl on me, I will scream, I will have to run," you would become phobic as well, and you would react the very same way as our subject. Such people are basically acting on what they believe, although it may be totally unfounded, and they may even understand that their thinking has no real merit. Because they believe these irrational thoughts, they act on them. In the end, changing the negative thought process will in turn change the result.

In the end, changing the negative thought process will in turn change the result.

STEP THREE GIVES YOU POWER

You'll need to create your page 2. Page 2 is the exact opposite of page 4. Instead of "Limited Beliefs," page 2 should be headed "Empowering Beliefs or Thoughts." Remembering that for every thought we act on, we get a result; if we act on an empowering belief, we will get an empowering result. In my seminar example, the empowering result would be to actually hold a spider. Take a few minutes and identify some empowering beliefs. This should be relatively easy. They will usually be the opposite of the information on your page 4.

My seminar subject's first thought on page 4 was "they are going to crawl on me." So what would be the positive or perhaps the opposite? The direct opposite of "they are going to crawl on me" would be "they are not going to crawl on me." But would this be entirely true? Yes, if we are using a rubber spider or a dead one, but I use a live spider for the demonstration. So I help my phobic subjects to an alternate thought for their page 2, such as "if it crawls on me that's okay." Why take this extra step? Because it is very possible that the spider would crawl onto the subject. The phrase "the spider will not crawl on me" would not be reasonable, and if we tried to use that and I got to the point where I was placing the spider on our subject's hand and it did crawl, we would immediately see a flying spider.

The next thought on the subject's page 4 was "I will scream!" Now this thought is something we can control (unlike a spider crawling), and we'll do it with a direct opposite thought, which is "I will *not* scream." Next was the thought "I will have to run away." Again, this is something that can be controlled directly, so the next thought on page 2 should be "I will not have to run away, and I am in control."

LOGIC MATTERS

Even though limited beliefs might logically be judged as absurd, they are still in control, and you will need to call upon logic in order to change them. If your new, empowering beliefs are absurd, the power of logic to help you affect change is eliminated. Your new empowering beliefs must make sense and be logical.

Even though limited beliefs might logically be judged as absurd, they are still in control.

The last thought on my subject's page 4 was "They are going to attack me!" This one could be tricky. The opposite would be "They are not going to attack me." This may or may not be true. If I happened to have a pet spider that's never harmed anyone in the years I've owned him or has never attempted to hurt someone, then I could confidently use the phrase "the spider is not going to attack me."

Unfortunately, some phobias aren't nearly as controllable, so the response must be reasonable and practical. For instance, if someone is phobic of dogs and his negative thought process says, "Dogs will attack me," we can't really say, "Dogs will not attack me." Some dogs do attack people. Perhaps we could say, "Not all dogs attack, and I will get near dogs that I know are friendly." It takes some common sense to effectively take what's on our page 4 and make an appropriately inverse, empowering statement for our page 2.

Don't get hung up on the phobia angle here. This can work on *any* behavior or belief you want to change.

From the beginning, I have told you I'd be giving you tools. Although the Four-Step Process itself is a big, powerful tool, I've discovered another tool, a phrase that people can add to their page 2 as a booster statement. The phrase is simply "No problem." The target is to make page 2 our real beliefs, which will take the place of our page 4 Limiting Beliefs. If a person already believed that something was no problem, it would be no problem.

At this point, we are now ready to start work on making real, measurable changes.

Although the Four-Step Process itself is a big, powerful tool, I've discovered another tool, a phrase that people can add to their page 2 as a booster statement. The phrase is simply "No problem."

Up to now it's been relatively easy. Figure out why you want to change, or at least why you think you want to change, identify the negative thoughts that are preventing you from changing, and reverse the negative thought to positive.

Many years ago I recall reading *Psycho-Cybernetics* by Maxwell Maltz, M.D., F.I.C.S. He spoke about the nervous system and how it can't tell the difference between imagination and reality. In clinical trials, people who practice something vividly in their minds can often improve as much as those who practice in reality. It's a great book full of scientific references and published findings on the topic. What's important is that understanding this fact can be incredibly powerful if you know how to apply it!

In addition to this revelation, it's common knowledge that as humans we usually take the course of least resistance. Combining these two premises allows me, in my live phobia reversals—and anyone else working through the Four-Step Process—to take the easier path of imagining overcoming an obstacle as a first step toward actually overcoming it.

In the live seminar as I am working with my candidates, I now ask them, "Assuming it's your goal to hold this spider, which one would you prefer to hold? An imaginary one or a real one?"

The answer is obvious, they always want to hold the imagined spider because that's the course of least resistance. But can we really be effective by having them hold an imagined spider? Most definitely!

Rather than cite the clinical trials in Maltz's book, let's do an informal experiment of our own. Imagine for a moment that my fingernails are long and I am going to run them along a dry chalk board. That description alone causes some people to cringe. That's because the nervous system often can't tell the difference between imagination and reality. For those who reacted to the fingernails on the chalk board, you basically painted a picture in your mind, and although it wasn't real, you still reacted. Your nervous system reacted the same way to the imagined scenario as it would to reality.

The nervous system often can't tell the difference between imagination and reality.

By preparing, training, and programming the nervous system you can prepare, train, and program your mind for the real world. Here is a simple example to help grasp the principle. Let's say you were by yourself in a room and I snuck up, just a few inches away from you, and yelled, "Boo!" If you're like most people, you'd jump, or scream, or have some other startled response. But what if I started with a discussion and told you that, in a few minutes, when the lights are out, I'm going to yell "Boo!" and suppose that I repeated this description several times? If you closed your eyes and imagined the scene, then when the lights went out and I really did yell, "Boo!" your nervous system would manage your startled response differently. You'd react far less dramatically—if you reacted at all.

In my live seminar, I want to train people's nervous systems and minds, so that they can slowly alter their responses, which will eventually help alter their thinking, and eventually they will hold the spider.

By preparing, training, and programming the nervous system you can prepare, train, and program your mind for the real world.

I have them focus on page 2 (Empowering Beliefs) and specifically on the No Problem belief. I tell them that I am going to ask a question and no matter what the question is, the response must be "no problem." For emphasis, I even test them at this point. I say, "I am going to ask you a question, and your answer will be what?" They reply, "No problem."

"Okay, here is the question . . ." (as I pull their hand toward me) I say, "In just a moment, but not now, I am going to put a spider in your hand. Is that a problem?"

At this point, if they are deeply phobic, they will have a very difficult time saying, "No problem." There will usually be a long pause before it comes out, and when they say, "No problem," it doesn't sound convincing. Their body language telegraphs that it is a problem, even though they verbally said it was no problem.

In actuality, when they say the words "no problem," they are lying. But are they starting to change? Absolutely.

JUSTIFICATION FOR INTENTIONALLY LYING TO OURSELVES

Let's first address the lying. The person in this example has *never* said, "No problem," about holding a spider. For the past 20 or 30 years that he has been plagued with his phobia, if someone had asked him to hold a spider, he has never said, "No problem." In fact, his response would be completely the opposite. We know from his page 4 how he would react: "I will scream, I will have to run away, they are going to attack me." And now he is saying, "No problem." Although he is lying and using positive thinking, he is already making slow improvements, because this is something that he would have never been able to say in the past.

When we say the word "lying," we don't mean it in a deceitful way. The "lying" in this context simply means we are saying something opposite from what we feel or believe. Often, what we feel or believe is not reality or truth, and is solely based on emotions. It's these emotions that control our lives, and we have become accustomed to being a slave to them. By lying, we are starting to fake the brain out. And while we're far from done, it is at least a start. Proponents of positive thinking stop at this point, so true change can never happen. Changing the negative words on page 4 to positive words or statements on page 2 and speaking these new beliefs and statements out loud is just an ingredient like the raw eggs. Fortunately, you're in the middle of an example of the right way to weave positive thinking into a larger, complete solution.

> *By lying, we are starting to fake the brain out. And while we're far from done, it is at least a start.*

Still, we can't forget that positive thinking is like spray paint on rust; it doesn't last long. This positive thinking, "no problem" response won't last a minute for a person with a deep-seated phobia. But all you need is a moment in order to get started in a new direction.

At this point, you'll want to add two more tools to your page 2. The first is the thought "When my feelings are not in harmony with my goals, ignore my feelings." This command is powerful, because it pulls together the various steps of the Four-Step Process.

The first part says, "When my feelings . . ." What feelings are we talking about? These are the feelings from page 4, all the negative feelings we experience. Next, ". . . feelings are not in harmony with my goals, . . ." What goals? These would be the goals on page 1. "Why I want to change this behavior?" This is what it's all about. The goal. What we specifically want to change. And last, ". . . ignore my feelings!" If we don't learn to ignore these feelings on page 4, the only alternative is to reward them. Rewarding negative behavior digs our grave deeper and deeper. It's got to stop, and this Four-Step Process stops it dead in it's tracks. Using intellect in this way allows us to progress. We can begin to overcome the negative feelings that arise in the Four-Step Process by ignoring them.

Unfortunately, most people are slaves to their feelings. If our (habitual/negative) feelings are not in harmony with our (positive) goals and we keep rewarding them, we will never make changes in our lives. The reason it is frequently so difficult to make changes is that our (preprogrammed bad) feelings keep getting in the way.

Most of us have been taught from Day One not to lie, and understandably so. Overcoming the negative feelings about lying to yourself in this process will be helpful in making your way past the limiting feelings. Obviously, this will be a challenge.

The reason it is frequently so difficult to make changes is that our (preprogrammed bad) feelings keep getting in the way.

Imagine that we are together in my office and I ask you to jump on my desk and show excitement and say, "Wow! This is great!" Would you feel uncomfortable doing this? Sure.

But now let's say I give you a million dollars, and I ask you to do the same thing. Would you feel more comfortable doing it? I would think so. In the first example, you didn't feel like doing it. So in effect you did something opposite from what you felt. Your feelings may have told you something like,

"This is stupid. Why would I want to jump on this desk?" Now that you are on the desk jumping with false excitement you *really* may think that it's stupid. Your actions are the opposite of your feelings, and it's uncomfortable doing things that are in conflict with our feelings.

Anytime you try to behave or act the opposite of how you feel, you feel as if you are lying. So if we've been taught not to lie, we'll jump off the desk and reward the feeling, "I feel that this is stupid. Get off the desk." Yet staying on the desk and faking it will force new behaviors to the point that we won't feel stupid.

Anytime you try to behave or act the opposite of how you feel, you feel as if you are lying.

In a sense, our normal state of being is like a bumper car. We get hit from the right, we go to the left. We get hit from behind, we go forward. No control whatsoever. When we start with page 2 (Empowering Beliefs), we are at least starting to add brakes to our bumper car.

Many times, we'll feel sad, so we act sad. When we feel happy, we act happy. What makes it so challenging to feel sad and act happy? The moment you try to act happy when you feel sad or jump on the desk when you feel it's stupid, you experience discomfort. Anytime you do something that's opposite of how you feel, you think consciously or otherwise that you are lying. Then you conclude that your behavior is wrong, and you go back to being sad. Unfortunately, this just rewards and reinforces the negative feelings on our page 4.

The second tool to add to your page 2 is this: *"Feelings change last!"*

This truth illustrates why making changes can be so very difficult. As you work on making changes, you'll find that the first and easiest things to change are the words. Moving from negative beliefs or words on page 4 to the positive words on page 2 was simple. Nothing to it. Positive words then positive thinking.

Recall as we say the positive words from page 2, which at this point are opposite from how we feel (page 4), we don't believe them. We say things like "No problem," and feel the problem is still a problem. So words change first, feelings change last.

As you progress and try to ignore or fight the negative feelings, you will still have a strong tendency to want to reward the feelings on page 4. You must use logic and understanding of the process to hang in there, because these negative feelings don't change right away. They change last. And it's especially difficult because we are constantly bombarded with the struggle to ignore our feelings when we've been rewarding the negative feelings for years.

You'll want to use your understanding that feelings change last, in order to give you an extra mental push to keep hanging in there long enough for the negative feelings on page 4 to fade.

And they will. When your feelings finally change, you will have adopted new feelings and rewired your brain.

You'll want to use your understanding that feelings change last, in order to give you an extra mental push to keep hanging in there long enough for the negative feelings on page 4 to fade.

Keep in mind that when you start this process, you believe everything that's on page 4. This is the root cause of your problems and the reason that changing can be so hard. After converting page 4 messages to page 2 statements (we turned them into positive thinking), the next real challenge is to get ourselves to believe what's on page 2. If we don't understand how and start making steps toward changing the negative beliefs, then everything on page 2 is nothing more than positive thinking. Alone, positive thinking never works, so stay tuned in to its role in the Four-Step Process and don't get caught up exclusively in positive thinking.

CHECKING YOUR NEW WIRING

When you actually affirm that your new, page 2 beliefs are real and your old, limiting beliefs are gone, you'll be able to make quantum leaps in your life. But when you first go through the Four-Step Process you'll want to know how to confirm that you've accepted your new belief. We need to build this up more before giving the answer. So how do you know that you are no longer believing what's on page 4 and you are starting to believe your words on page 2? How do you know when you've actually bought a belief? The simple answer is that you've truly changed when your feelings match your words.

Don't ever forget that. Your target must be to get your feelings to match your positive thinking. Then and only then will you see an immediate and consistent change in your behavior, and *this* is how you *know* that you've bought a new belief!

You've truly changed when your feelings match your words.

MAKING FEELINGS CHANGE

We now need to focus on getting those feeling to match our words. The answer to doing this is in the statement "When my feelings are not in harmony with my goals, ignore my feelings." We have already started to ignore our feelings by the use of words. The next step is how we say those words. We must say them as though we believe them. This is what will help fake the brain out.

Suppose that I am on stage doing this demonstration and for the first time I ask the subject to say "no problem" in response to the question "I'm going to put the tarantula in your hand. Is that a problem?" If the subject responds, "No problem," that is a great start. But how they say it is vital. Many of them look and sound like ventriloquists. Their brain picks up on that, and it knows they don't really mean it. It's time to fake it out some more.

I never know the audience members that I bring up on stage. I do know that they are lying when they say "no problem" for the first time. I want them to demonstrate to me how they say "no problem" and really mean it. Here's how that's done.

I proceed this way. "I am going to ask you another question, and this time I want you again to say 'no problem.'" To make sure they've really got it, I repeat the statement. As I pull their hand over, as if to prepare them to hold something, I say, "In just a moment, I am going to put a million dollars in your hand. Is that a problem?" They always say, *"no problem!!!!!"* and they really mean "no problem." The words are correct, how they are said and the person's body language must also say "no problem" as well.

My goal now is to get them to say the "no problem" exactly the same way for the spider as they did for the million dollars. At this point, I do everything in progressive steps. Once I feel that they can say "no problem" to holding it, and it's the real "no problem," we step up to letting it crawl on them and then touching it. This can take a while, and because I'm not writing a phobia reversal text book, we'll skip some of the little reinforcing steps I do in my live encounters.

Each tangible step must first be approved by the nervous system. In other words, if they can't touch the imagined spider with the nervous system, they are unable to move to trying to touch the real one.

What do I mean by touching the imagined spider with the nervous system? Suppose that I say, "We are going to imagine touching the spider, is that a problem?" If the subjects are still struggling to say "no problem," they are by no means ready for the real thing. I just keep working with them on their nervous system until I see feedback that they are ready to move on to the next little step.

Once we are at the point where all the positive statements on their page 2 sound great, it's time to attack our candidates verbally and see how they hold up. For instance, let's say we are playing football and you and I are on Team A, playing against Team B. Imagine if you could make yourself invisible and then sneak over to Team B while they are in their huddle planning what to do on the next play. You then take that information back to your team. What kind of advantage would you have? A great advantage. Plan on winning!

You would now be equipped with this same advantage using the Four-Step Process. You know what your opponents are thinking, and, more important, you know what they are going to do. In football we call this cheating, but the example illustrates how you will want to cheat to make progress in the Four-Step Process. Here you'll stop feeling guilty about cheating on your opponent once you understand who your opponent is in this example. Your opponent is you from your own page 4 beliefs.

You will want to cheat to make progress in the Four-Step Process.

Now I'll prepare my volunteers for the attack. I will fire at them everything from their page 4. "Ha-ha, they're going to crawl on you! You're going to have to scream and run away! The spider is going to attack you!" As I am saying all of this I want them to counter attack me and even interrupt me. They can't allow page 4 to rent space in their head.

They need to respond, "So what if it crawls on me. I won't scream and run away. I'm in control. This spider is harmless." This trains the mind to prepare for the attack. Why is this important? Because it's going to happen. Their page 4 has been with them for years if not decades. The moment they try to move forward, page 4 is going to attack. I prepare them for the internal attack, without the real spider, so they can develop the pattern to counterattack their page 4 trash of limited or negative feelings.

If they weren't trained to counterattack in a controlled situation, without the real spider in front of them, page 4's thoughts would flood their thinking, and they would quickly (or possibly immediately) begin to reward those thoughts, and never make any progress at all. When you see someone put up vigorous verbal resistance to their old page 4 in favor of their new page 2 beliefs, change is obvious and is definitely being made.

Often, the next point to tackle is what to do in order to make the change long lasting. I have heard for years that it takes 21 days to change a habit. I have no idea who came up with that, but it's ridiculous. If this were true, everyone could change everything, and it would only take 21 days of a little practice. Each person is different, and it could take minutes to change. I help people reverse life-long phobias in well under an hour. Now maybe if you've never made your bed in your life and you want to get into that habit, you could remind yourself to do it every day for three weeks, and then it might become a new habit. So I suppose it could work that way. But if your problems are bigger than wrinkled sheets, or if you don't want to dedicate three weeks and you're committed to change in a big way, other tools (like the Four-Step Process) can frequently help you make lasting change in no time.

Making the change permanent is the ultimate success. We've all heard of the expression "the yo-yo syndrome." We get results for a short period of time then we regress, up and down. This behavior is very pronounced in relationships, diets, and finances. Page 3 will help solve this problem. One reason permanent results are so hard to reach is because too often we focus on changing the results. That sounds logical, but that only gives us temporary change, if it works at all.

The reason the change is temporary is because we may not have taken the time to identify the limited thought process or processes that are causing the limited result. For change to be permanent, we must first change the thought process. Remember, for every thought we act on, we get a result. While this is being accomplished through the Four-Step Process, we need to make the change stick.

Making the change permanent is the ultimate success. We've all heard of the expression "the yo-yo syndrome."

STEP FOUR: CREATING YOUR PAGE 3 CEMENTS THE CHANGE

You start making things stick on page 3 (New Positive Feelings and Experiences). For many people, their page 3 is quite the opposite from their old or negative feelings and experiences. It's like people who get a dent in their new car, and all they talk about and focus on when they get into their car is the dent. They forget about the entire car. Unfortunately, it's the negative feelings and experiences in life that can suppress any good feelings we may have had in the past. This causes us to constantly live in the past. The goal now would be to totally reverse this: allowing the positive feelings and experiences to suppress all the negative ones.

The best way to do this is to write them down. The reason it's very important to write them down is that if we are not able to specifically and regularly focus on these new positive emotions and feelings, the negative ones will win. The key here is to constantly build one new positive feeling or emotion on top of another until they suppress the old, negative ones that were on our page 4.

One of the ways I do this in the phobia reversal is, once I successfully get our candidate to touch an imagined spider, I train the nervous system to get her to respond in the following way. Referring to the imagined spider I say, "In just a moment, I am going to take your finger and touch the real spider, and the moment you touch it you are going to say, 'it's so soft.'"

The goal now would be to totally reverse this: allowing the positive feelings and experiences to suppress all the negative ones.

Then I take the finger and gently touch it to the palm of my hand (the imaginary spider), illustrating the point that soon a spider will really be there. The moment she touches the palm of my hand, she says, "Oh, it's so soft." Is this person lying? Absolutely. We know that because of the manner in which she is speaking. Once subjects master this, we are now ready for the real thing.

Here it comes. Now it's time for the real spider. With some reservation and with my assistance in holding a finger or hand, the subjects reach over, touch it and say what they practiced: "Oh, it's so soft." Most of the time, they will immediately react and look at me and say, "Hey, it really was soft." The moment they say something like this without being prompted, they are not just saying words. Now they believe. These words have new meanings now. They say its soft, and they truly believe it now, due to real experience.

Your page 3 will need to be loaded with positive experiences, new realizations, and so forth for the Four-Step Process to work and cement new beliefs in place of old ones. As you continue to try to change, before you confront more of the same thing, keep looking at your page 3 to relive your positive experiences, emotions, and feelings. Make sure you write them down in enough detail so that if you were to read your notes months from now, you would still be able to relive the feelings (not just recall the thought) and use those feelings as your spring board to keep going forward. It's okay to include negative things on your page 3, but make sure you end up with positive results. You might write, "I had to admit, I was forcing myself, and I felt very uncomfortable, but I did what was on page 2 and it was great. I did this, and this happened to me. It was exhilarating."

Your page 3 will need to be loaded with positive experiences, new realizations, and so forth for the Four-Step Process to work and cement new beliefs in place of old ones.

It's okay to record the fact that these feelings or thoughts are negative. In fact, the negative feelings and thoughts can be even more empowering, because they highlight the contrast between your before and after behaviors. It shows how much you have overcome.

FOUR STEPS, FOUR PAGES . . .
MAKE THAT THREE PAGES

Arguably the biggest challenge anyone can have is a deep-seated phobia. These irrational beliefs are so overpowering that they can control and potentially ruin most aspects of the phobic's life. (Phobias are the extreme example and you need to remember how this works on any behavior you want to change.) And using the Four-Step Process to reverse a phobia is an incredibly powerful example of how anyone, with the right tools, used in the right way (sometimes with a coach for extreme situations), can overcome any negative belief system and rewire one's own brain. The Four-Step Process can be used to overcome any obstacles or failings and turn your life around. Elsewhere in the book, you'll see more ways to apply the Four-Step Process to your own problems and challenges.

One last little tool in the Four-Step Process always makes

me smile. When you work through all of the four steps and look back over your four page, find where it says, "Feelings change last" on your page 2. If your feelings have changed and you're done with the Four-Step Process, throw away page 4!

SUMMARY

- The Four-Step Process can be used in business and your personal life to help you master your own circumstances and outcomes.
- The Four-Step Process is a way to rewire your own brain.
- Each step of the process is represented by a notebook page, but you don't necessarily create the pages in the order you use them.
- Step One is to research which counter-productive behaviors must change and why you must change those behaviors.
- Step Two is on page 4. List the beliefs you hold that limit you in this situation.
- Step Three is to create your page 2 containing empowering beliefs or thoughts that are opposite of your limiting beliefs.
- You don't necessarily need to believe the beliefs you write down on your page 2; you just have to define beliefs that are empowering and that overcome the limiting beliefs of your page 4 current beliefs. You will grow into these new beliefs.
- The new empowering beliefs should be logical, even if your limiting beliefs are illogical.

- As you attempt to grow into your new beliefs, remember that feelings change last.

- Step Four is to create page 3 and populate it with a list of positive things you've experienced now that you have developed your new beliefs.

- Once you've fully changed your feelings to the new page 2 feelings, throw away your page 4.

Chapter 14

FEELING IS BELIEVING

There are several truths I want you to understand about emotions. First, it's natural to be controlled by our emotions. Second, emotions are powerful enough that they can, and frequently do, drive our behavior to reach results that are consistent with our beliefs. Third, with the proper coaching and insights, most people can use their intellect to master their emotions and turn them into guided tools that help us achieve our goals. In order to understand your emotions and how to control them, instead of letting them control you, you need to start by understanding their origin.

We are naturally controlled by our feelings. That's because usually, what we feel is a result of what we believe, and our beliefs, coupled with our feelings (emotions) create our reality. If we feel scared, we act scared. We feel sad, so we act sad, and so on. Have you ever known someone at work who thought someone else (or everyone) didn't like him or was out to get him? Even if that wasn't reality in the beginning, by constantly acting defensive and looking for a conspiracy where none exists, he creates situations that result in people not liking him in the end. His emotions drive his actions and create their negative reality.

A big part of the process of using emotions and feelings as a tool is to use exercises that make us especially aware of our emotions. After one-on-one consultations with clients, I usually tell them that they'll feel as though they're walking on egg shells for a while. That's because they become so aware of their emotions and how environmental factors evoke emotional reactions. Normally, people just react to stimuli, and their emotions "just happen." To date, their emotions haven't ever resulted from a conscious decision to react in a particular way. Simply being aware of each emotion feels strange in the beginning, but it's a critical first step to controlling them.

Normally, people just react to stimuli, and their emotions "just happen."

Unfortunately, our feelings can occasionally lead us (to react or behave) in the wrong direction. As I mentioned earlier, most people are slaves to their feelings. This is not good if our feelings are not in harmony with our goals, and then we reward those feelings. Remember, goals are usually set intellectually (as they should be). Whenever we reward feelings that are inconsistent with our goals, this prevents us from being able to attain those goals. Imagine, though, that our feelings were always consistent with our goals, and we rewarded *those* feelings. We would be able to accomplish incredible things, not to mention that we would always feel great! Even though that's never the way emotions work automatically, it is possible to be aware of our feelings. Then we can choose to keep the feelings we like and reward them, and the feelings that aren't consistent with our goals can be ignored or discarded in favor of more positive, productive feelings.

If you don't make a conscious effort to stop the natural progression of rewarding whatever feeling automatically arises from environmental circumstances and your natural reactions, then you'll be a slave to your feelings, good or bad, 'til the day you die. Obviously, that's not a good thing. You can't claim to have emotional control if you are regularly and easily influenced by your feelings.

In the beginning, it can be almost overwhelming as you start tuning in to your emotions. As humans, we have a vast number of different emotions that we experience every single day. We are capable of experiencing thousands of emotions. Most are subtle and can pass in an instant, while others consume more of our time and attention. An exercise I believe helps people to realize this, is tracking their emotions in a journal for just one day. Surprisingly, most people will write down 10 to 20 emotions when in fact they may experience hundreds. Try this yourself, and see how many you can recognize.

You can't claim to have emotional control if you are regularly and easily influenced by your feelings.

After you have completed this exercise, take another few minutes to review your list and choose which of the feelings you recorded are feelings that you'd like to experience again. Write an "A" (for "Again") in the margin by each one. Next write a "P" by each emotion you experienced that you think helps you to be more productive. You will find that there is a vast difference between the emotions you'd like to experience again and emotions that are most productive. And keep in mind that emotions don't necessarily need to be positive in order to be in the productive category. Finally, any emotion which is neither positive or helpful should get a designation of "N" (for "Negative") in the margin. If you find any emotion is both negative and helps you be productive, write both letters (P and N) beside them, but circle the letter with the biggest influence. The reason for this is because you don't necessarily want to avoid or eliminate emotions that may be somewhat negative but that help you reach your goals. The main thing at this point is simply to track your emotions and evaluate them.

For example, let's say you wrote down that you experienced the following emotions: anger, upset, excited, content, hurt, happy, fulfilled, challenged, scared, stressed, motivated, rejected, and unstoppable. If asked which emotions help you to be productive, most people wouldn't include feelings like scared, angry, stressed, or rejected. The truth is, these can be productive feelings even though they appear negative. Of course, this will depend on the situation and your goals, but these can be leveraged as empowering emotions.

If we chose to react by giving in to these emotions (reward them in a negative way), then they are *not* productive. But if we use them as leverage, often they can motivate us to go forward and make changes, so that we don't have to experience those feelings again. For example, when people procrastinate, they are able to enjoy whatever positive feelings they can during the present moment instead of the less preferred work of accomplishing a particular task. Putting off the task will eventually cause pain, but procrastinators will continue to put off the task until the negative feeling looms so large in the near future that they simply must drop everything else and tackle the task right away. If they could learn to experience that pain a week or month before that drop-dead deadline by immersing themselves in their future bad feelings *before* they really happen, they would be able to stop procrastinating.

> *When people procrastinate, they are able to enjoy whatever positive feelings they can during the present moment instead of the less preferred work of accomplishing a particular task.*

Procrastinators need to feel pain in their very near future before they make a move, even though it's occasionally too late for that particular project. People like this are really a slave to their feelings. And it's not just a matter of switching focus from the present okay feelings to the future pain they'll experience as a result of procrastinating. In order for this fix to work, procrastinators have to immerse themselves in the bad feelings of the future, and do so long before they are *really* imminent. They have to concentrate on all of the bad things and the feelings they will experience in the future.

Procrastinators have to immerse themselves in the bad feelings of the future, and do so long before they are **really** *imminent.*

I've already explained how the nervous system can't tell the difference between imagination and reality. This concept explains why imagining future pain, as completely as possible, can help a procrastinator get things done in the present.

I'll share with you the thought process that I use to master my feelings and convert my controlled feelings into a tool I use to constantly take action toward my goals. You'll find that one of the keys to this exercise is to literally stop and think as opposed to being like a bumper car that just goes where it's hit. When I think about something that I know I need to do, but I don't feel like doing it, I immediately think about the consequences of not doing it. This wasn't automatic until I practiced this technique for some time, but now it is. This thought process is just a start. There's more. I must not only focus on the consequences, but I must imagine and try to *feel the pain* or experience the feeling that would eventually cause me to jump up and get the job done.

It's the feeling that we normally experience when we wait so long that finally moves us, only in this case, we choose to feel it before it's too late as a means of self-motivation. The longer we delay the feeling, the more we procrastinate. Focus on future pain, and bring it into the present, and then let your nervous system react as though the pain were already here.

The longer we delay the feeling, the more we procrastinate.

When parents can help their children recall feeling pain, they can get their children to listen and respond more quickly to their requests. Have you ever seen parents tell a child to do something, and the child just looks at them or simply ignores them? The parents raise their voice and still no response. Now the counting begins. "Don't make me start counting. Now pick that up. One . . ." Still no response from the child. "Two." Still no response from the child. And some parents even take the opportunity to teach fractions . . . "Two and a half . . . Two and three fourths."

It's usually between two and a half and three that the child finally makes a move. The child finally listens to the parent but only after waiting forever, and now both parties are upset. This could have easily been prevented.

Consider what happened. The reason the child didn't take action from the first command or instruction was because the child knows that the parent doesn't mean it. They know there are no negative consequences such as punishment or a spanking at the first initial instruction. They don't mentally feel the pain yet. They have been programmed by the parents so that when they give an instruction the child doesn't have to listen or obey until Mom or Dad starts counting.

POWER TIP

Adopting the right perception helps develop the right attitude.

The parent starts counting, and the child still doesn't act because it knows that the spanking or the real yelling doesn't happen till Mom or Dad gets between two and a half and two and three fourths. It's right at that point that the child has been programmed that there are imminent consequences for not behaving. The child imagines and feels the pain from past experiences that Mom counted to nearly three before punishment.

Parents will say at times, "If you don't do this, you are going to get spanked," or they will mention some other type of punishment. The child may nod its head in acknowledgement but never seem to listen. Having a child think about the consequences is not as motivating as if it were able to feel the consequences. Remember, it's the feeling that often controls us.

Let me share with you a true and perfect example of this. I was riding in the back seat of a friend's car. His wife was in the front passenger seat, and I sat behind her. The son, who was about five years old, sat to my left. This little boy was like most little boys. We had been in the car for several hours, and he was starting to act up. He was doing something that annoyed his father. "Son, if you don't stop doing that, you are going to get a spanking." The father's admonishments were totally ignored. "Son, I've told you to stop that. Do you want me to spank you?" And still his requests were totally ignored.

Having a child think about the consequences is not as motivating as if it were able to feel the consequences. Remember, it's the feeling that often controls us.

At this point, I leaned over to the boy and said to him, "Don't you realize that if you don't stop what you are doing that your daddy is going to spank you?" He smiled, looked at me, and said, "Yes." I asked him, "So why do you keep doing it?" His brilliant answer was "I forget the pain."

Daddy only reminded him about thinking about the spanking when he said, "If you don't stop doing that, you are going to get a spanking!" But if dad could get him to recall what the pain felt like as opposed to thinking about it, his son would immediately obey. How do we know this? Because once Dad starts reaching around the back seat the son associates that look on Dad's face and that hand coming around to meaning real business and some physical pain. He knows what he is going to feel next. If Dad created a pattern so that the moment he tells his child to do something, the child should associate the feeling of pain immediately, the child would likely then not wait for the counting to begin.

This explains the reason that we often do the same things over and over again, knowing the outcome would not be the best thing for us, yet we keep repeating negative behavior after we've told ourselves we'll never do that again. People do this in diets, relationships, and with spending money. Some get into nasty relationships or just ones they don't like and eventually get out of them. Usually, after the other person hurts them, they say, "I'll never get into a relationship like that again." And after six months or so they are in the same type of relationship again or even back with the same person.

In this relationship example, people feel the climax of pain during the breakup. They can remember what this pain feels like for some time. During this period, they say and follow through with thoughts like "I won't have anything to do with you."

Then as time passes by, they will remember that pain happened, but they forget to remind themselves to *feel* the pain again. Forgetting this kind of pain is a part of the natural healing process, but unless you make yourself remember various (especially painful) aspects of the negative relationship you're doomed to repeat the bad relationship again. It's at this point that people get caught in a vicious cycle. Back and forth . . . Back and forth.

Forgetting this kind of pain is a part of the natural healing process, but unless you make yourself remember various (especially painful) aspects of the negative relationship you're doomed to repeat the bad relationship again.

If a person is caught up in this pattern and decided to put an end to it, he must remember and *feel* the pain that prevents him from getting involved in the relationship. Recalling the pain in full detail has to start at the moment he just considers the relationship again. He needs to avoid allowing something to cause him to forget his past pain. He must learn to recall everything about that pain, up to its climax when he broke up. If he can do that whenever he needs, he can break the pattern.

If a person is caught up in this pattern and decided to put an end to it, he must remember and **feel** *the pain that prevents him from getting involved in the relationship.*

Sometimes when I describe this method of evoking powerful emotions based on strong negative feelings from the past, people say that they can't imagine being able to do it. And even if they could, it wouldn't be a strong enough emotion to dramatically affect their behavior. I'd be willing to bet that most people already do this exact thing, but they aren't necessarily triggering the thoughts and feelings because they *want* to.

Consider that you experienced a specific situation as long as 10 years ago that caused a deep-seated feeling of animosity or resentment toward someone. It might be an acquaintance or even a former friend. Even after 10 years has passed and you've never seen each other, strong negative feelings survive, and neither you or the other person cares to make amends.

Now imagine you happen to see each other. You can bet that the exact emotions you felt 10 years ago will immediately boil up inside each of you, and you might even be ready for a fight on the spot. Here we have feelings that haven't been a part of our lives for 10 years, but they pop up again, just like yesterday.

I'm sure you've experienced something like this before. Maybe it wasn't a fight, maybe it was a positive emotion. It could have been a chance meeting with an old classmate, and you picked up with your friend right where you left off years ago. Smells and old songs can be powerful memory triggers that bring back a flood of feelings and emotions that have been buried or forgotten for years. If you can do it without trying, all you need to do is develop a system that allows you to call on this ability to use it to your own intentional advantage.

In order for the bigger system to work, you must learn to create a pattern of behavior that causes you to respond consciously. To do this effectively, you have to work on creating a momentary delay between a situation or thought and the feeling it gives you—and always go through this process *before* you respond. By being in tune with your various emotions and knowing they are something that you can control and manipulate, you will be able to affect your own response, and usually (you'll get better with practice) keep your actions in harmony with your goals.

It's important that you be able to pretend to feel and then learn to react as opposed to being a slave to your feelings. It's incredibly empowering to break away from being controlled by your emotions and even more empowering when you can make your emotions fuel your own best interests.

Now that you understand the concepts of how and why to control your feelings, it's important that you have a formula you can use to take control of your feelings. This formula assumes that you have already defined your goals (it helps if they're in writing) before you encounter a situation wherein you would normally just react.

It's important that you have a formula you can use to take control of your feelings.

---

(1) Begin by identifying and interrupting feelings and related knee-jerk reactions. Become aware. You must learn to become extremely aware and in tune to your feelings. What's worse than feeling negative or depressed is not knowing why we feel a particular emotion. I used to wake up feeling happy some days, and other days I would wake up feeling depressed. It was frustrating because I couldn't put my finger on why I had these feelings, good or bad.

If you don't know why you are depressed (or happy) how are you going to be able to change the emotions? Not knowing the source of an emotion isn't just frustrating, it prevents you from being able to facilitate emotional changes too. On the other side of the coin, if we don't know what's making us feel happy, how are we going to be able to duplicate happy feelings in the future at will, so we can keep being happy.

As with all of the material in my programs, this situation presumes that the person who is depressed or unhappy isn't experiencing clinical depression, bipolar disorder, or a chemical imbalance requiring medical intervention. While some of my strategies even work for clinically diagnosed patients, I don't intend to claim that my strategies always work for everyone or that they are a replacement for medical treatment. In some cases, it is critical that patients stay on medication for the rest of their life. In some cases, people can eventually taper off their medication and resume a normal, balanced life with no additional medication. In either case, it's important to trust your treating physician(s), and if that requires a visit to other physicians for second or third opinions to feel confident in your treatment regimen, that's reasonable.

While some of my strategies even work for clinically diagnosed patients, I don't intend to claim that my strategies always work for everyone or that they are a replacement for medical treatment.

Having said that, the opposite is true as well. Some people who believe that they need medical treatment may just have a belief system that isn't willing to accept the possibility that they have control over their own behavior and emotions. It is my sincere wish that these people find a treating physician who sees through the patient's beliefs and prescribes nothing stronger than a placebo.

Incidentally, this is a big reason people turn to drugs and

alcohol. They use these chemicals to control their emotions and feelings. *Unfortunately, the control doesn't usually turn out in the intoxicated person's best interest.*

Some time ago, I made it a point to learn to master my emotions and figure out what made me tick. I've found one of the best ways to do this is to keep a journal of my day-to-day emotions. When you do this, you will begin to see patterns. Often, these patterns will give you hints or answers as to why you feel the way you do.

Use your knowledge from the previous chapter (the Four-Step Process) to help identify any limited beliefs that you have to a specific situation that might be causing you to over-react emotionally. For some people, they react the way they do to situations because of a simple limited belief such as "that's the way I was raised" or "that's how I've always done things." With someone who has those beliefs, it might be time to counteract with the belief that you can't change what you don't acknowledge. Just because you were raised a particular way doesn't always mean that way is right, at least with regard to this particular situation.

Once you've mastered that to a degree, look past the emotion at the apparent trigger and analyze that as well. Consider if your emotional trigger even deserves your reaction. Again, at this beginning stage you don't have to worry so much about the big picture and how to avoid negative emotions. In fact, avoiding or ignoring them isn't really the goal here. Your target should be to identify as many positive and negative emotions as possible and also consider their source.

If you can identify at least some of your major emotions and their triggers, you're ready for the next step.

Your target should be to identify as many positive and negative emotions as possible and also consider their source.

---

(2) Once you've become aware of your feelings, you need to stop the ones which aren't in harmony with your goals. Try to live according to the emotional motto "When my feelings are not in harmony with my goals, ignore my feelings."

Unlike suppressing feelings that you simply can't handle (which can lead to all kinds of problems and may even require professional help to overcome) "ignore my feelings" in this context means that you recognize what your natural reaction is, yet you've chosen intellectually that you aren't willing to empower those emotions to control your behavior. This distinction is a *big difference*!

I've found, in working with people and helping them with their goals, that most people don't think of goals as being defined as emotional. They associate their sales goals, career goals, lifestyle goals (house, car, marriage) with material acquisitions or lifetime milestones. It's critical that we tie our goals to emotions if we want to use the power of emotions to achieve them. It's our emotions and feelings that either move us or they don't.

If you have a material goal, try to redefine it in terms of the emotional reason you want to achieve that goal. Almost all people value their own happiness (as they well should). Realizing abundant happiness is a great goal. A great goal is to want more emotional control over your life. Another one is to want more passion and excitement in your life. Maybe you want to act more like a child and enjoy life more. Maybe you want to be more playful.

A great goal is to want more emotional control over your life.

These are all great emotional goals. As for material goals, try to categorize them under an emotional heading. An employment goal might go under the security emotional heading. A sales goal might fall under the heading of personal accomplishment.

So when a situation arises as part of daily life that evokes an emotional response—if you can identify it—you need to use your emotional goals checklist to see if the emotion associated with that situation is in harmony with your goals. Negative emotions usually breed negative emotions, and positive emotions usually breed positive emotions. Too often when we get depressed, angered, or upset, the emotion takes over to such a point we don't even realize it's happening.

If someone would figuratively (or literally) slap us and ask us about our emotions, we might be able to get a grip on the situation, but the natural tendency is to let ourselves get carried away. The moment this happens, we need to focus on the following considerations: (1) this is negative, and (2) why should I work on changing this? Your why needs to be a strong reason if your negative emotion is strong. You'll need to consider your motivations for change before you need to apply them to breaking an emotional cycle.

One of the possible whys might be that you want to be happier. You value your happiness. Maybe your why is that you want more emotional control over your life. Maybe you want to have more passion and excitement in your life. Maybe because you want to act more like a child and enjoy your life more. Maybe because you want to be more playful. Maybe your why is that you want to reach a particular employment goal, and managing this type of challenge is required on your way to that goal. This type of thought process helps you begin to put a stop to, interrupt, or break these patterns of negative feelings.

If we don't have emotional goals, what's going to stop us from allowing our negative emotions to keep breeding negative emotions? These go hand in hand. If you don't make it a goal to master your emotions, then they will master you. That must be one of your emotional goals.

This type of thought process helps you begin to put a stop to, interrupt, or break these patterns of negative feelings.

(3) Practice so you can turn this into a pattern of action (you should only act after analyzing potential outcomes). Interrupting certain emotions, especially the negative ones, can be challenging, so it may help you to pay attention to all of your emotions—positive and negative, large and small. If you're feeling great and positive and marching toward a goal with gusto, stop for a moment and consider the emotion. Don't make it go away, but consider it clinically for a while. Then, at some point during your day, try recognizing some simple negative emotions and feelings. Not the big, bad ones. Just pay attention to the little frustrating or irritating things that happen during the day. See if you can interrupt one of them for a bit of consideration or analysis. In the beginning you don't have to fully change your feelings, just learn to spot as many influencing emotions as you can.

See if you can interrupt one of them for a bit of consideration or analysis.

You should also try to identify why you react the way you do. Recall earlier that I said what I've often found to be worse than being depressed is not knowing what caused me to be so depressed. You almost always need to understand the source of your feelings before you can change them, so practice focusing on that too.

(4) Learn to identify feelings that make you take action and evoke them to move you toward desired outcomes. A great by-product of being in tune with your feelings and emotions is the fact that you will be able to identify the feelings that cause you to take action toward your goals and those that cause you to slow down or maybe even want to quit. You can either use these feelings to motivate you from a neutral state to a motivated, active state, or you can use them to replace nonproductive emotions.

Have you ever taken the time to stop and think about what feelings or emotions get you to take action toward your goals? This is different from what motivates you generally, although they usually work hand in hand. Wanting a new house or a better future for your family may be a motivating factor, but there are feelings associated with this that get you moving toward your goals. Take some time to figure them out. Then keep doing things to create those feelings again and again. Experiencing those feelings repeatedly motivates you to keep taking action.

Take a future feeling, bring it to now, and use it to achieve desired outcomes. For example, think of a better life or future for your family—something specific like a bigger house so all five kids don't have to sleep in the same room. Dwell on the joy that the new house would bring the family, and use that to motivate you to work harder or be more disciplined. Use those emotions to help you follow through and take action toward the short-term goals, which will eventually bring you to your larger house goal.

THE FOUR STEPS TO EMOTIONAL
CONTROL IN PRACTICE

Let's summarize by considering some ways to work with the nervous system to help us take action and move forward. Keep in mind that the nervous system can't tell the difference between imagination and reality. We can use this principle to induce feelings, both positive and negative, at will.

Here is an example. Let's say you're a guy who knows your wife would love to get some flowers from you but you don't have a habit of buying them. How can you encourage yourself to get flowers? First, acknowledge it needs to be done. Now *stop, literally, take a deep breath in . . . let it out slowly. Relax. Maybe even close your eyes, and think.* Don't think about why you haven't been doing this or that you should get flowers because she would love them. Consider what would have to happen or what has happened in the past, which made you feel rightfully compelled to buy her flowers.

The nervous system can't tell the difference between imagination and reality. We can use this principle to induce feelings, both positive and negative, at will.

This is where you daydream a bit. . . . Imagine going back to when you were dating and you brought her flowers. Now don't just think about when you did it, try to recall the feelings that moved you to buy the flowers. Picture when you bought them years ago. Try to relive those feelings of being in love and the appreciation you had for her back then. Get emotional about the experience. Remember how great it felt when you gave her the flowers? Remember how appreciated you felt? Perhaps those feeling aren't as intense now as back then. It's a human tendency. Go beyond the present, and try to relive your past feelings once again. You have this aced when you can literally feel those emotions again. Practice for a while until you really get it.

Now that you are experiencing the emotions and feelings, you need to reward them immediately. Take action. Make that call. Order the flowers, or go and pick them up. Now if this is really out of character for you, she'll wonder what you did wrong. Then again, maybe that's a feeling that you need to use to get more flowers for her in the future.

In many businesses, cold-calling and prospecting is a great way to dramatically increase sales. The problem is that most people hate it, in spite of the fact that it's a sure way to increase sales. You can use emotional control to get past cold-call avoidance.

The first step is to acknowledge what action needs to be taken. The answer is that we need to cold-call and prospect more. Second, stop, relax, and think. Consider the limiting beliefs that you are using that keep you from prospecting and cold-calling. Third, create the emotions that once motivated you or would motivate you to cold-call.

From my experience, many often wait till they begin to run low on money or it's the end of the month and they are not making quota, which could jeopardize their job. They wait until then to start cold-calling. If that's it, then that's the emotion that moves this person to finally get up and take action. Now, if they took this action earlier in the month and did a lot more of it, they would receive the financial benefits from it. And if they did it long enough and got enough benefit from early action, cold-calling will eventually be as natural to them as breathing.

So think about it already being the end of the month. Try to bring those feelings that you would experience at the end of the month that would motivate you (by force), and then act on them.

This technique is incredibly powerful for sales teams. They would be able to win more customers (and those great internal sales games) if they could master this.

Try to bring those feelings that you would experience at the end of the month that would motivate you (by force), and then act on them.

I can think of dozens of football games that were decided in the last two minutes of the game because everybody is moving as fast as they can. Sometimes no huddles. They throw the ball amazingly fast, and the teamwork runs like clockwork. Everything is happening fast and furious, and they're getting things done. The entire team has adopted a state of readiness and an incredibly fast-moving pace. Imagine if they could make that kind of teamwork happen at will, any time before the two-minute warning. It can be done but not many teams (football, sales, corporate) or even individuals push to achieve at these levels.

When you go from experiencing the motivating emotion, you have to make yourself take action to create a positive pattern. If you don't do these steps simultaneously, you will create an environment that will cause you to procrastinate even further. What I mean is that you never want to get to the point where you bring up the emotions that would cause you to act and then not act.

If you create the situation and follow through with appropriate, positive action, you begin to develop the positive pattern of how to manage and control your emotions. During this learning stage, if you allow yourself to not follow through, you have simply created a new negative pattern that's even worse than the original one because you've taught yourself a new way to procrastinate.

If you allow yourself to not follow through, you have simply created a new negative pattern that's even worse than the original one.

A new nonproductive pattern means that after a while your partner (the brain) won't assist you any further. You can look at it as bad programming. Then when you try this again in the future and you really need to take action, your brain will tell you, *Every time we play this game and I give you the emotions you're looking for, you never reward them, so why should I help you now?* You need to be disciplined while building your new pattern. While it's never a good idea to rely on willpower for the long haul, you'll need to make a conscious effort to create your new, positive pattern of emotional control. Everyone is different, and it may take you a great deal of practice, or just a little, before you start to develop your own pattern of channeling feelings and emotions to your benefit.

Consciously applying the four steps above is the pathway. Practice is the key. Now all you have to do is choose to open the door to controlling your feelings and emotions to your benefit.

If you don't feel sufficient emotions when you try to evoke the ones that motivate you, keep working on it. In the meantime, it may help you to act as though you do feel the emotion you want, and to take action accordingly.

I'd like to wrap up the discussion of this new discipline by sharing how I have used it to accomplish personal and professional goals.

When I hear about someone having a heart attack due to bad eating habits, I think about myself as if I were in the same situation. If a doctor did a check up on me now and told me that if I don't change my eating habits, I'll have a heart attack within the next six months, I'd do something about my diet. Most people would.

Unfortunately, that's what it takes for most people. When it's gotten really bad, when I hear about people getting sick or dying due to poor health, I focus on what I would feel like in their position. I regularly think about what I would lose if I don't take care of myself. This is what I do on a regular basis to keep me on track to eating right and staying healthy. Take the time to live the feeling then reward it. Create a habit or pattern.

Years ago, and for some time, I wanted to learn to fly helicopters. As you can imagine, the process is quite expensive. I really needed as many ways as possible to motivate myself to work hard so I could afford to take lessons. Just hearing the sound of a helicopter got me excited. The smell and feel of the leather. The smell of the fuel. I would go to the airport and watch a helicopter start up and get an emotional thrill. Then I would make the association of that excitement to my work, and I would get right back to the office and hit it hard again. I would even record the sound of the helicopter starting and put it in my stereo alarm clock so that instead of waking up to an alarm, I would wake up to the sound of a helicopter.

It's like being like a little kid in a toy store. Once a kid is in the store and sees all the toys and touches them, he gets a lot more hyper. He can feel what it would be like to play with those toys any time he wanted. Learn to be a kid again. Imagine the excitement, but make sure to channel your excitement into doing something so that you take action that brings you closer to your goal.

Learn to be a kid again. Imagine the excitement.

SUMMARY

▌ It's natural to be controlled by our emotions.

▌ Emotions are so powerful that they can, and frequently do, drive our behavior to reach results that are consistent with our beliefs.

▌ With the proper coaching and insights, most people can use their intellect to master their emotions and turn them into guided tools that help us achieve our goals.

▌ You must first recognize as many natural emotions as possible.

▌ Initially, you won't be able to control your big, overwhelming emotions, but you can start by controlling the little ones.

▌ Negative feelings can sometimes drive you to positive actions.

▌ Using your imagination to bring future pain into the present can be the trigger you need to overcome procrastination or other bad behavior.

▌ Interrupt your reactions as often as you can identify them.

▍ When your feelings are not in harmony with your goals, ignore your feelings. (Fly by your instruments/beliefs as mentioned in Chapter 8.)

▍ Practice interrupting emotional responses to create the pattern of action and *decide* to follow through only on feelings that are in harmony with your goals.

▍ Learn to identify feelings that make you take action, and evoke them to move you toward desired outcomes.

▍ If you interrupt a bad feeling, and don't replace it with a new, productive feeling, you will create an equally bad, new, nonproductive pattern.

▍ Using emotions and feelings is one of the most powerful ways to direct yourself to your goals.

Chapter 15

Play Games with Your Mind instead of Letting Your Mind Play Games with You

B y now, there should be no argument that so many of the challenges we experience in business and in life are little more than a mind game. Our minds are constantly playing games with us. Sometimes, the mind games are more apparent than others, but they are always there, whether it's a fear of success, rejection, easily being angered, feeling intimidated, inferior, or feeling stupid. Our emotions are at the center of the factors that influence our behavior by playing with our minds. Negative, unproductive things happen when we let the mind play games with us. We have to learn to be mentally tough and learn to take and maintain control. We must learn to direct our emotions to get the results we want. In effect, we've got to learn to play games with our minds instead of letting our minds play games with us.

We must learn to direct our emotions to get the results we want.

Mind games is a good way to describe the Four-Step Process, mental vertigo, positive thinking, and a host of other systems of thinking and reacting we've discussed in earlier chapters. It's ultimately beneficial to discover as many ways as you can to keep yourself in control of your emotions, so that you can use them to move you toward your goals.

When we are too easily susceptible to external stimuli, we are basically controlled by other people or other things. I've seen many apparently successful people who have no emotional control. They are constantly yelling at their staff, and they are very unpleasant to work with. They are ticking emotional time bombs. This affects their focus and their personal happiness, not to mention the happiness of people who have to be around them. So mastering the ability to play games with your mind is something we can all work on, no matter where we are in life—rich or poor, young or old.

I've shared quite a few concepts and even some specific things you can do to take back control of things that are influencing you in counterproductive ways. For every method I've described, there are others I haven't even mentioned. I'd like to share a mind game I've been able to use to my own benefit over the years.

One way I try to keep things from renting space in my head is to be on stage. It's the same on stage term that actors use. In fact, I understand that Disney uses this term with their employees. They teach their cast members, as they call them, that the moment they are in the public eye, they must be on stage. They are going to act happy and smile and be friendly even if they don't feel like it.

One way I try to keep things from renting space in my head is to be on stage.

So if you feel that you are letting something rent space in your head, if you are not careful, you're going to reward that negative feeling with some type of negative action. But if you fight it, similar to your page 2 in the Four-Step Process, by being on stage and acting that way, acting as if you weren't affected by it, at least you're fighting back. Really, you're playing games with your mind instead of letting it play games with you. You are doing something to take back control.

I remember years ago, when I was preparing to take my commercial helicopter check-ride with the FAA (not for a business, just as another personal goal). Before you can qualify for this license, you must be able to fly the helicopter to a specific standard. That takes lessons, time, and money. The next step is to prove it to the FAA by actually flying with them. If you're up to the proper standard, you pass and you can become a commercial helicopter pilot.

POWER TIP

Setting the goal is important, but following through makes it a reality.

I had to book my appointment nearly two months in advance, and there were no other openings for the next few months due to the examiners' schedule. If that wasn't bad enough, I had to drive three hours to the airport where the examiner was, and use their helicopter. The night before my exam I started coming down with flulike symptoms. I woke up the next morning with a fever of about 102 degrees. I could barely move. If I canceled my flight, I would lose money, and I would have to reschedule months later, *plus* I would have to keep flying the helicopter regularly until then to maintain standards, which, at over $200 an hour, adds up real quick. I was sick, and I wasn't in any shape to drive, much less fly a helicopter to commercial standards.

I had my wife drive me three hours to the airport. The moment I got out of the car, I was on stage. I met with the examiner and told him nothing of how I felt. I wouldn't because I was on stage. He finished with the oral exam, and we were off to the helicopter. After we finished my check-ride he said my standards were up to instructor level, and I passed the test. After signing the necessary paperwork, I got in the car and off stage. In fact, I nearly collapsed, and I fell asleep immediately. I would certainly not recommend to anyone to take on stage behavior to this extreme, but I knew my limits, and I knew what would happen if I didn't push them. It also goes without saying that the examiner usually has much more experience than the person he is flying with, so even if I couldn't stick it out, he would have been able to take control.

Pushing to these extremes isn't for everyone, but it certainly gives you added confidence when things are not quite so extreme. More than once, I've stretched my mind and body to see what I can do. I know how much more I am capable of as a human. As part of an especially hectic period at work, I have pushed myself to go straight for 36 hours without sleep. At times, I have to go 24 hours straight due to some of my scheduling. Because I've forced myself to stretch to 36 hours straight, 24 hours is nothing. It is truly amazing what we are capable of when we don't let things rent space in our head.

Pushing to these extremes isn't for everyone, but it certainly gives you added confidence when things are not quite so extreme.

Here is another example of how you can play games with your mind. We've all been in social situations when we knew someone was talking about us and it wasn't necessarily nice. Maybe you've even heard someone say, "They were just talking about you and saying all kinds of stuff. You should have heard what they said!"

When something like this happens, the normal human tendency is to ask what they said. Some people just won't stop until they find out. All it does is feed their insecurity and make things worse. It is such a nice feeling when you know someone has said something negative about you and you don't even bother asking what was said. It's a real feeling of control. Some people let things like that eat them up for years. Besides, we usually make it worse than it really is anyway. Be on stage. Don't ask, and just move on.

Taken to the extreme, some people might even be a bit paranoid or overly sensitive, and in a similar situation there may be no discussion about them at all, but they just *think* there is. If they ask someone to "tell me what they said about me," then they are letting their own thoughts rent space in their head. They have some serious work to do on their emotional control.

On a more light-hearted note, have you ever told children to clean their rooms, and the response you get is "I'm tired. I don't feel like it." Next time that happens, immediately respond by saying, "Okay, are you in the mood to go to the zoo" (or some theme park they've been dying to visit)? If you're standing in the doorway, you had better move because they're headed straight to the car! Their mood seems to change almost miraculously.

Feelings and moods can change instantly, but most of us change them subconsciously. If you were in bed half asleep and felt really tired, how fast do you think you could change your mood and become very energetic and move like lightning? The answer is very fast. If someone yelled, *"Fire! fire!"* how quick would you move?

Feelings and moods can change instantly, but most of us change them unconsciously.

In this case, though, you had to wait for someone to yell "fire" before you moved. My point is that we have the capacity to instantly change our moods and feelings. Think about how often you have used your moods or emotions to stop you from taking action toward your goals. It happens daily! Simply being more aware that you are largely in control of your moods and emotions opens a world of opportunities for moving forward toward your goals.

At times when I do get upset, I don't allow my mood to let me cancel an appointment because I don't feel like it. I push and stretch myself. The emotions and feelings usually change soon after, and often I later forget what I was upset about in the first place.

Once again, if you think that what I'm suggesting is that simply feeling positive and slapping a big, silly smile on your face will change your life forever, go back and start the book over. You missed something. All I'm suggesting is that, once you recognize that you can be more completely in control of your feelings and emotions, and if you fully understand them and your motivations, then you can redirect your emotions and feelings to help you reach your goals. There's a *big* difference.

Once you recognize that you can be more completely in control of your feelings and emotions, and if you fully understand them and your motivations, then you can redirect your emotions and feelings to help you reach your goals.

So take the time to identify what might be playing games with your mind and, more important, what you can do to change that. I hope that this chapter enables to you continue to be much more aware of your historical and environmental influences and how you let them affect or not affect your day-to-day activities. This is just one more way you can learn to play games with your mind instead of letting your mind play games with you.

SUMMARY

▮ Negative, unproductive things happen when we let the mind play games with us. We have to learn to be mentally tough and learn to take and maintain control.

▮ We must learn to direct our emotions to get the results we want.

▮ When we are too easily susceptible to external stimuli, we are basically controlled by other people or other things.

▮ One mind game you can use to overcome present circumstances is to be on stage no matter how you feel.

▮ Everyone understands that they would sprint for the door if someone yelled, "*Fire!*" but very few people use their knowledge of their own motivation to accomplish things on a day-to-day basis.

▮ Once you recognize that you can be more completely in control of your feelings and emotions, and if you fully understand them and your motivations, then you can redirect your emotions and feelings to help you reach your goals.

Chapter 16

ACKNOWLEDGE
THE JOURNEY

L ife's a journey, not a destination. Most of us have heard this statement before. For me, early in life I personally never really understood it. As I've shared with you previously, I used to set myself up for failure because of my inexperience and my irrational optimism. I'd set goals and give them deadlines, but I never seemed to reach the goal by the deadline, so I'd get discouraged and want to quit.

When I was young, I had a burning desire to reach my business and personal goals. I still have a fire for my goals, but my understanding of my journey toward those goals is different now. First of all, I reached many of my goals later than I initially expected. Then, as I started reaching many of my business and financial goals, I found that it wasn't enough. I was not only unsatisfied, I was disappointed. I thought that reaching a goal would have a bigger payoff. This is a tendency for many of us, and it can be very unhealthy if this attitude isn't adjusted by a balanced viewpoint.

Remember that I told you about the times when I would take other people flying with me to the Caribbean in the first plane I owned. It had seating for only four people and was a single-engine airplane. Every time we'd land back in the United States to clear customs, we'd park our airplane at the airport next to a larger one and I would hear, "When are you going to start flying one of those?"

Then when I did buy a larger, twin-engine aircraft and we'd be flying back, this time with more people on board, we'd pull up to the customs ramp and park beside a Learjet . . . sure enough I'd here it again: "When are you going to start flying one of those?" Then, when I started flying Learjets, I parked beside a 747 and you guessed it, same old question. When does it stop?

This illustration gives us insight into human nature. If we're not careful, we'll program ourselves to never be happy. We must come to a realization that our life is a journey. If you are constantly pushing for the destination, when you get there you may find it very disappointing, because the satisfaction of reaching that goal isn't enough to make you happy for longer than a moment. If you think goals are your destinations, you will eventually stop striving for them, because the payoff is rarely as good as you imagined when you made it a goal in the first place.

If you are constantly pushing for the destination, when you get there you may find it very disappointing.

You have to remember that there will always be someone more beautiful, richer, thinner, faster, younger, more popular. The key is to learn to enjoy the present while you focus on the future and never forget the big picture of your journey.

Two years before he died, millionaire tycoon J. P. Getty said, "Money doesn't neces-

POWER TIP

Knowledge is power, but only if you use it!

sarily have any connection with happiness. Maybe with un-happiness." One of my millionaire mentors, Dan Bagley, used to tell me that if you don't know how to handle money, all it will do is make you comfortably unhappy.

There will always be someone more beautiful, richer, thinner, faster, younger, more popular.

One billionaire had a series of unhappy marriages. When asked what gave him the most happiness, even in view of his great wealth, he thought a while and answered, "A walk along a good beach, and then a swim." That is something even the poorest person can often do free of charge!

Thinking like this may go against your grain. If you're caught up in struggling for more money or possessions, you may tie those possessions to your definition of happiness. That's because our society programs us to reach the next milestone, and messages from the media and advertisers re-inforce the idea that our happiness will be tied to our posses-sions or our goal achievement. And the programming starts when we're young.

As a kid, I remember never being tall enough to get on that ride at my favorite theme park. I hated that little silhouette guy at the ride entrance. I remember going back a few years later and being tall enough. It was a great feeling. But I had bigger goals than the theme park ride. I was just dying to be a teenager. That wasn't enough, though. Next, we want a dri-ver's license, then a car, then marriage, then kids, and then we can't wait till they leave the house. These days don't we wish we could be kids again? Play, play, play . . . have fun and no responsibilities.

It's great to be motivated to strive for your next goal. It's important to never be complacent about everything, because that's the first step to becoming a couch potato. On the other hand, if you can't ever get joy from your accomplishments along the way, that can be equally discouraging. If you can move away from thinking of goals as destinations and consider the bigger journey of your life, you'll be more likely to experience more and greater happiness and, ironically, you'll be motivated to set and achieve more goals and be happier, even before you reach each goal or milestone.

Mastering this can be one of the keys to true happiness. I recall years ago a friend asked me if I would love to own a Gulfstream Jet. New, they sell for over $40 million. Sure. Who wouldn't love to fly around like that? But I told him it wasn't one of my goals. I've got to stop somewhere. I regularly move up the aviation ladder with new plane and helicopter goals, the business ladder with new company and staff growth plans, and the personal ladder. I also recognize that every goal requires that a price be paid, and I know that the price I would have to pay to own a new Gulfstream Jet would not be worth it to me.

This balance took me years to master. I remember going to one of the many Sandals Resorts in the Caribbean. Wow! They are impressive resorts. A tropical paradise can really affect your perspective. Because I know the owner of the resort and frequently work with him and his company, I have a personal connection. I used to get discouraged going to his resorts because I thought that I could never accomplish anything like what he had. It can be overwhelming when you see your own accomplishments compared to the achievements of a billionaire.

Every goal requires that a price be paid, and I know that the price I would have to pay to own a new Gulfstream Jet would not be worth it to me.

I've learned that I should compare my accomplishments to my own goals and simply use the impressive accomplishments of others as proof that nothing is impossible. I wouldn't ever say that I'm complacent, but I do try to take time regularly to consider how many of my goals I have achieved. That big-picture view helps me acknowledge the journey, and it gives me a sense of happiness and satisfaction along the way. That can be just the kind of thing you need to recharge your batteries. Having the right big-picture focus can be just the thing you need in order to keep your goals and to prevent the opinions of others about your accomplishments from renting space in your head.

I've learned that I should compare my accomplishments to my own goals and simply use the impressive accomplishments of others as proof that nothing is impossible.

In earlier chapters, I've asked you to write down things like emotions that help you be productive and those that are unproductive. I've had you write down goals for various exercises too. Now it's time to take a truly broad view of your motivations, emotions, and goals, and to consider the times in your life when you've been truly happy. I'm not just talking about laughing at a stand-up special on TV that features your favorite comedian; I'm talking about the kind of happiness where you find yourself smiling during an experience that's not necessarily funny, the kind of experience where the smile is on the inside, the kind of happy that seems to touch on emotions like content, satisfied, and truly optimistic, the kind of happy that compels you to thank your creator for all you've been given.

Get out your pad and write "Truly Happy Times" on the top of a new page. Then close your eyes and remember the times in your life when that deep level of satisfied happiness filled you from the inside, and jot down when and where you were.

Usually doing this exercise can help most people get a bit

more in touch with their sense of satisfaction and gratitude. If you're looking through the prism of recent tragedy or clinical depression, your present attitude can be distorted by over-powering negative feelings, and you may be looking at those great, happy times as strictly in your past and out of your grasp because of whatever has you down right now. If that better describes your current view, try focusing on the fact that, even though true happiness might *seem* to be outside your grasp, you have a book full of tools to overcome challenges and one or more of them will certainly help you pull yourself out of your present, to a more fulfilling, positive future. Even if the feeling evades you right now, keep in mind that there will be a time in the future when you will feel better and closer to experiencing that deeply satisfying sense of happiness again. Use your analytical mind to acknowledge your present mood, and then admit that things won't always stay the way they are.

Even if the feeling evades you right now, keep in mind that there will be a time in the future when you will feel better and closer to experiencing that deeply satisfying sense of happiness again.

Once you can wrap your thoughts around a few of those times when you experienced true happiness, consider that you will benefit if you can regularly revisit this state of mind.

Caution: If you believe that revisiting your truly happy times is a solution in and of itself, then you've missed the point entirely. This exercise is a tool you can use to reframe your perspective of your journey; it's absolutely *not* a way to fix problems.

People are empowered by all kinds of different thoughts and drive toward goals because of these various triggers. Focusing on this kind of happiness can be one of those motivating triggers, not to mention that it will help you put your daily journey in perspective. It's fine to live one day at a time and focus on the present, but regularly considering your own big picture is also a necessary perspective to maintain.

If you think about your life's work and your journey as a literal cross-country trip you might take, you should understand that simply living day to day with the "we'll cross that bridge when we come to it" attitude can be less than clever planning. Sure, you can't actually cross a bridge before you reach it, but if you look at a map and plan your journey, you might find that there are restrictions on the bridge you plan to use and you'll need to take a different route. If you don't periodically look at your journey from this perspective, you can waste years of your life taking a path that leads to a dead end road that you didn't know was there because you have just been living day to day.

At the risk of taking this analogy too far, you will also want to get updated maps every year or two. New roads get built, and old ones are closed. Current maps are critical to your journey. What I mean is that you should consider your journey regularly, and plan some time every year to look at the big picture of your journey.

Not only will this help you stay on track toward your goals, it can be amazingly rewarding to see how far you've come.

You should consider your journey regularly, and plan some time every year to look at the big picture of your journey.

It's easy to get caught up in the drudgery of daily work, so taking the big picture into consideration regularly can help you stay on course, and if you've set some medium, and long-range goals, you'll frequently find that looking at this big picture will become a source of that transcendent happiness we talked about earlier.

Life's a journey, not a destination. Nice thought, but it's far more useful when you acknowledge the journey and use that realization to make sure you stay on the best path for you.

SUMMARY

- If you are strictly goal-focused and ignore your journey, when you reach a big goal, your achievement will be hollow.
- Life is a gift, goals are milestones, the path should be cherished as well as the milestones.
- Part of determining appropriate goals is understanding what your life will be like as you strive for those goals.
- Enjoying life between milestones should be a goal too.
- Often, incredibly wealthy people get great enjoyment from things that are free.
- Happiness can help you along the way toward your goals, and the trip to your goals can make you happy too. It should be a win-win situation.
- Occasionally stepping back from your goals to acknowledge your journey can help you see if you're still on the best path to the goal. Maybe there's a new road to your destination that you'd otherwise miss.

Chapter 17

IT'S TIME TO RE-EDIT YOUR VIDEO

Whether or not you've ever been involved in the television or movie business, undoubtedly you've seen a behind-the-scenes program about what it took to create a particular movie. On TV talk shows, there's somebody every single week talking about the months of filming on location, followed by months of editing, that all went into making their latest film. Consider the hours and hours of filmed material that hits the cutting room floor, all to make a 90-minute statement in a movie theater. The choice of scenes the director keeps and the many more he decides to cut, all evolve into a finished film that conveys the director's vision of a story he wants to relate to the viewer.

Consider the hours and hours of filmed material that hits the cutting room floor, all to make a 90-minute statement in a movie theater.

The same kind of thing happens on a much smaller, more accelerated scale when it comes to TV news and 30-minute entertainment shows. There are far more minutes of captured video than ever make it to air. That's because the director (or reporter) has only a limited amount of time to tell the story, and she decides what is important to the story and what can be edited out. Whether or not you realize it, you've got a video of your own about your life, and you play it for yourself now and then.

Everyone's life is absolutely filled with years of experiences, stories, and emotions, reflecting humor, tragedy, boredom, intrigue, solitude, celebration, and desire. Then consider that your story is still unfolding every single day. Most people haven't sat in an (imaginary) editing suite for hours, reviewing their life's video (experiences) in order to create the most motivating, uplifting, thoughtful, intelligent, comprehensive, forward-thinking, compassionate, insightful, and compelling video possible. And even fewer people have considered that they have enough video on file that they could probably make a few variations of their video in order to tell their story the right way whenever they need. Unfortunately, most people just watch clips of whatever videos are laying around, and the editing is deplorable. It's truly junk television.

And even fewer people have considered that they have enough video on file that they could probably make a few variations of their video in order to tell their story the right way whenever they need.

The great news is that this book has walked you through dozens of ways you can help yourself have a fresh perspective on your life. When you consider your life and all that you're going through, and when you're interrupting your negative emotional patterns, having this additional way of looking at your life (the video) can be helpful.

If you find yourself watching tragedy-centered videos all day, pop in a tape of an uplifting movie to shift your mood. Okay, enough of the video analogy. I'm sure you get it.

I'd like to take the opportunity, here at the close of the book, to share a few stories that could easily have been in earlier chapters. I've saved them for here because, as you read the stories, if you consider how having the right video playing can change your state of mind while everything around you

POWER TIP

A farmer cannot harvest the farm by thinking about it in his mind.

seems to be going crazy, it will give you even greater insight into my reactions at the time and encourage you to use the video technique for yourself. And there's even a story about how I've helped my nephew create a little video he has been able to play to help himself over the years.

Let me start by telling you that I have the greatest respect for law enforcement officials all across the country. They have a difficult job and work hard to help people and keep us all safe. Yet in spite of the hard work and obvious peril most officers experience regularly on behalf of the citizens, there are occasionally those who seem to have attended a different kind of police academy.

I recall one multiday trip, flying to California from Florida to do a segment for a national television show. On the way to California, I had two speaking engagements, one in Alabama and the second in Wichita, Kansas. I woke up early in the morning and landed in Alabama, did my speaking engagement and then flew out to Wichita. It made for a long day, but I took my good friend Dominic with me for company and because he has some experience flying, which would let me take a bit of a break now and then. Oh, one more thing. It will help if you know that Dominic and I were both born in Jamaica, but his skin is light brown.

We finally landed in Wichita after our flight from Alabama, and we didn't want to wait for the rental car company to deliver our car, so before I landed the plane I radioed ground operations to have our rental car pulled up the moment we landed. (I do this all the time.) Once the car pulls up, it's customary for the line person who dropped the car to assist you with any luggage.

> *In spite of the hard work and obvious peril most officers experience regularly on behalf of the citizens, there are occasionally those who seem to have attended a different kind of police academy.*

I didn't need to be anywhere until Monday morning, and since it was only Saturday I wanted to take a few minutes and organize the airplane. While I was still sitting in the cockpit, I yelled out to the young man that I appreciated him bringing the car planeside, but we didn't need any further assistance. I reasoned that there was no sense in having him wait for 10 minutes or more for me to organize things. He seemed curious and tried to peek inside the cabin of the airplane. I didn't give it much thought at the time, but I'm sure he couldn't see much because we had all the windows covered up during the flight. I always keep my windows covered with sunshades except when flying, but because no one was in the plane with Dominic and me, we left most of the windows covered so that there would be one less thing to do when we got to Wichita.

After straightening up the plane, Dominic and I got into the car and drove to our hotel. Before arriving in Kansas, I had made an appointment with one of the local airplane manufacturers to visit their plant on Sunday. Dominic and I were interested in looking at some of their jets. On Sunday, as we were leaving the hotel for our tour, we both noticed that the hotel seemed to be really quiet, especially the wing where we were.

After we came back from our jet plant tour, we decided to

relax a bit and rest up for the speaking engagement the next morning and our flight to California for the television program. It was only the middle of the afternoon, but we both fell asleep and were jolted awake by a knock on the door. I was in one of those sleepy states when you hear the door, but you're not sure what's real and what's part of your dream. Dominic was a bit more awake than me so he opened the door. He woke me up, and I was greeted by three DEA agents, standing by my bed with 9 mm pistols. As I am not accustomed to waking up with DEA agents, I was caught a bit off guard.

I was greeted by three DEA agents, standing by my bed with 9 mm pistols.

Three armed agents. One seemed to be obsessed with his microphone. He kept talking to more agents outside. I'll call him Mr. Microphone. What was amazing to me is that they had even more agents outside. How many DEA agents does it take to bring down a public speaker and his friend?

The Special Agent in charge told me that they had solid reason to conclude that we were big time drug smugglers and he proceeded to pull out a warrant from a judge to enter my aircraft. Mr. Microphone looked over to the special agent as he began the questioning. (I guess he's called special agent because he got to ask the questions.)

He looked at me and asked me point blank. "Do you have drugs on your airplane?" I said, "No." Then I followed up with, "Seriously guys, this is a joke, right? I'm going to make a phone call. I know who put you up to this."

They wouldn't let me make a phone call. I still thought this had to be a joke, but their guns looked pretty authentic. He got a bit louder as he asked the same question again. "Do you have drugs on your airplane!?" I looked at him and said, "When I landed I had no drugs on my plane. Now if you guys planted drugs on my plane, then I have drugs on my plane." (Maybe I've seen too many movies).

For future reference, if a DEA agent ever asks you if you have drugs on your plane, the best response is *not*, "If *you* planted drugs on my plane then I have drugs on my plane."

For some reason, they just didn't like my response, but at least it was true.

They wouldn't stop with the questions. They where absolutely convinced that they had two drug smugglers who were headed straight to jail. They searched the hotel room. They checked the bathrooms, the mattress, you name it. Nothing! Two things came to mind at this point: (1) Thank goodness I didn't have to clean up hotel rooms for a living; and (2) frustrated DEA agents are less friendly than you might hope.

After more questioning, they discovered that my friend and I are both originally from Jamaica. I'm not sure why the location of our birth has anything to do with why we were in Wichita that day, but for them it seemed to answer their question about why a Caucasian and an African American could be friends.

Add our Jamaican origin to the fact that the type of airplane I was flying at the time is very well known for trafficking drugs because it can hold so much weight, so I think they felt they had an airtight case.

My friend and I are both originally from Jamaica. I'm not sure why the location of our birth has anything to do with why we were in Wichita that day, but for them it seemed to answer their question about why a Caucasian and an African American could be friends.

It was about then that it finally clicked as to why our hotel seemed so deserted. I later found out that the DEA had been hot on our trail shortly after we arrived at the hotel. Someone tipped them off from the airport. "A black guy and a white guy didn't want any help at the airport and their windows were covered. Oh, and they're in a plane that's great for carrying drugs." That was the full extent of their tip about what just had to be smugglers. What other explanation could there be?

To this day, I can't get over the manpower the Wichita office of the DEA dedicated to a tip from a suspicious airport employee. They had so many officers and agents tracking us that you would think we were the culmination of some huge, nationwide drug sting.

To this day, I can't get over the manpower the Wichita office of the DEA dedicated to a tip from a suspicious airport employee.

They actually shut down an entire wing of our hotel for nearly 24 hours, and the DEA had us under surveillance. They had followed us to the plant to see the jets. As the questioning continued, they wanted to know what we were doing looking at jets. I guess I seemed a bit young to be looking at jets. They had to be thinking, *"Normal people can't afford jets so these guys must be trafficking drugs."* Talk about limited beliefs.

The agents had told the hotel staff that we were big time drug dealers and employees had reason to fear for their lives. *Not only have I never done drugs in my life*, these guys were unnecessarily scaring the heck out of the hotel staff with unfounded and outright lies. The hotel staff was instructed to call the agents and tell them *anything* we asked or spoke to them about. That's how they knew we were going to see the jets. We asked hotel staff for directions, so they had to tell the agents.

As the questioning continued, they separated Dominic and me, and drove us each to the airport. It was easy for Dominic and me to keep our stories straight because *we actually were just a couple of friends on our way to do a couple of speaking engagements and a TV show in California!* Our families go way back.

When we got to the security gate at the airport, even more agents came out of nowhere. We approached the gate at the airport perimeter. Now, I guess it's just my sense of humor and a feeling that I needed to lighten the mood a little. I looked over to Mr. Microphone and asked, "You wouldn't think it would be too funny if I tried to open the door about now and go for a little run, would you?" For some reason, his sense of humor wasn't at quite the same level as mine that day.

Now I've seen cop shows on TV, so I know this is the point where things are supposed to get really dramatic. Dominic and I both arrived, and we were driven planeside. They asked us one more time, "Are you sure there isn't anything you want to tell us?" I said, "Yes, who scratched up my airplane?"

An agent said, "The dogs did." "The what!?" I asked. The agent continued, "We sent out a drug-sniffing dog and he went berserk because he smelled drugs, and that's how we were able to get this search warrant. Are you sure you don't have drugs on the plane?" I insisted that I didn't.

They asked us one more time, "Are you sure there isn't anything you want to tell us?" I said, "Yes, who scratched up my airplane?"

You could tell that every agent there was just waiting to haul out bales of something so they could stand in front of cameras on the Wichita nightly news and talk about the months of work that went into this huge takedown.

After opening the door he saw my huge stash of . . . CDs and tapes. Box after box of seminar handouts and not even the slightest hint of anything drug-related. Needless to say, the special agents didn't feel too special after all that. We didn't even get an apology. Nine months later we *did* get a check for the damage the dogs did to the paint, though.

I just went to Wichita for a speaking engagement, to look at jets, and to relax a little on the way to California. And my adventure turned out to be something I could add to my video collection, *literally*. I was able to have fun with all this in the local Wichita media and talk about my little visit. I did all kinds of interviews, but unfortunately the press only heard my side of things because the agents got a little amnesia and wouldn't say anything to the media. To this day, I wonder if that drug-sniffing dog ever got in trouble. Maybe they put him at a desk job for a few weeks.

Not even the slightest hint of anything drug-related. Needless to say, the special agents didn't feel too special after all that. We didn't even get an apology.

I think it's important to allow yourself to be flexible and adaptable to change. As circumstances change, you may have to re-edit your video again. As we experience new and different things in our lives, we must change. For instance, people's values change the moment they have a child. They look at things from a different perspective from before. Adjustments in thinking and lifestyle need to be made.

As you enter a new financial level, higher or unfortunately lower, you again have to make adjustments in your video. Whenever you begin to experience things that you never thought of, the quicker you can adjust to your new circumstances, the better off you'll be.

Successes are truly built on failures. One of the most powerful and rewarding benefits of not letting things rent space in your head is the fact that we all travel through uncharted territory and we are bound to fail regularly along the way. Not letting things rent space in your head means that you will be able to invent, create, and master new ways of doing things.

A perfect example of this is the space travel. Decades ago, it was considered absurd to imagine we could go into space. Then people made the trip to the moon. More than once. Did people lose their lives to get there? Of course, but the never-give-up attitude allowed us to persevere. The improvement of space travel and the quality of the technology used to get there has often improved, based on accidents and failure. But dwelling on failure didn't launch a single ship. Adaptation and innovation did.

I recall years ago flying back from the Caribbean in a rented airplane and losing engine oil pressure. Oil started spewing out from the engine's cover onto the window. I could barely see a thing. I was over land, and it was obvious that I would need to abort the flight, and soon too. I was able to find a makeshift runway. It was a road between a barricade and an active road. I glided in. After an experience like that, your mind can really play games with you. Quit or keep flying? I must admit, at the time I was a bit skittish about getting back on the horse, but I refused to quit flying. I flew the next day.

Some people will never fly again after an incident like that. My thought was *I've spent so much money, time and effort learning to fly that it would be a waste for me to quit now.* In retrospect, it made me a better pilot. (It also motivated me to buy and maintain my own helicopters and planes and rent as little as possible.) My training was expensive, but part of that training was how to handle emergencies. I was able to use my training. It paid off.

Some people have family members or friends who have died in a plane crash. They have chosen to never fly again. I've heard of people having a family member die in a car crash, and they now walk to work and will never drive a car. These are examples of people who haven't re-edited their video. It takes effort, and it's a continual process.

I've heard of people having a family member die in a car crash, and they now walk to work and will never drive a car. These are examples of people who haven't re-edited their video.

If you agree with this, *do something about it!* The last thing I want you to do while reading this book is to nod your head and say, "Yep. I agree." What I share with you will only benefit you if you follow through. That means you are going beyond agreeing to a belief, and an active belief is what ultimately gets results. What can make it so challenging to re-edit our thinking when things get tough is the fact that we have a tendency to get wrapped up in the emotion of the moment, and we find it hard to see beyond the problem.

Maybe you've been told to remember your successes. That's a good idea, but there is something that works a lot better. A successful tool in being able to re-edit your video is to stay focused, not just on your past successes, but on your specific past failures that you turned into successes.

Remembering our successes does help, but focusing on what it took to get there is even wiser. This is what the third step, "New Positive Feeling and Experiences," in the Four-Step Process does for you. Remember that I told you to write down new feelings and experiences *and* the negative feelings that you had experienced before the new ones. That helps you remember your path, though painful at times, to your success. We all love to hear stories about the underdog winning. That's what page 3 does for us. Often, the more painful the ride to the top, the more memorable and motivating it becomes.

There's a simple way I've used this principle to help my young nephew grow up with a healthy sense of self-esteem and an "I can do it" attitude.

> *Often, the more painful the ride to the top, the more*
> *memorable and motivating it becomes.*

I've been putting my nephew, Steven, in the cockpit and letting him actually fly since he was about 5 years old. When he was about nine, I let him help with radio communications, and I had him talk to the air traffic controller. We were on a runway, ready to take off from an airport that didn't have a control tower. At small airports like this, you just make an announcement on the radio of your intentions, and if there is anyone in the area, they will acknowledge. Then you continue broadcasting your intentions (where you are on the runway, direction of travel, and so forth), so that everyone in the vicinity can use that airport safely.

As we were about to take off, I told Steven what to say, and it was a bit lengthy. With engines running and ready for departure, he looked at me and said, "I can't say all that. I can't." I said, "You can do it, we are on the runway. You've got to." He pushed the microphone, and he did it.

Immediately after takeoff I congratulated him. Later on in the flight, I reminded him what happened. I said, "Remember when we were about to take off, and I asked you to talk on the radio? What did you say?"

I got him to repeat what he had said first. "I can't," he said. Then I asked him, "But what happened?" He said, "I did it!" And I reinforced his success once again with more congratulations.

Then I asked him, "If you ever think you can't do something, you what?" "I can!" he said proudly. We've added a clip to his video.

To this day, I still remind him of his radio accomplishment. I go through the very same scenario. In fact, I did it this past weekend when we were together. I try to do this at least once or so a month. And I do it out of the blue. The timing has absolutely nothing to do with a particular situation where he is trying to tackle something challenging. Oh, I'll certainly remind him of it then too, but I've been reminding him of this for years anyway.

I plan to remind him of this for decades to come. It's a constant reinforcement that he couldn't, yet he did! He now has an example of a triumph over "I can't," which he can use to prove it. It seems quite simple, and it is, but it is also very powerful. This helps him take control of future thoughts that might want to control him.

So what about you? Are there things in your personal or professional life that you are not doing that you should be doing? Is there some negative experience you've had, or someone else had, that's renting space in your head and preventing you from moving forward?

It is my hope that this book has given you countless ideas and tools to assist you in re-editing your thinking on your journey. To truly master this, you have to be willing to make changes and keep an open mind. Trust your own intuition, and use emotions and feelings to your advantage, rather than allowing them to control you. Keep identifying areas in your life that you want to improve and do specific things, even small things, to get the results you are looking for.

Trust your own intuition, and use emotions and feelings to your advantage, rather than allowing them to control you.

The success that you see others have, couples married for 30 or 40 years who truly seem to be happy, financial successes of business professionals and sales superstars, these things don't happen overnight. They're part of a bigger plan that's been in play for a long time. Just make sure that you're always looking for some way to chip away at your plan. Don't let a day go by that you are not improving. Do something every day to work toward your goals. Keep working on mastering even greater control and don't stop re-editing your video.

SUMMARY

- The collection of your life's experience is too over-whelming to consider every day so when you take a minute to define yourself, you summarize.
- If your whole life were a film, you'd be working from a five-minute highlight reel.
- Choosing better clips from your life for your video can change your whole outlook.

Chapter 18

Energizing Your Life in Spite of the Obstacles— Pulling It All Together

Regardless of your path so far in life or your plans and future goals, even your dreams, there will inevitably be obstacles. It's not normal for most people to develop a comprehensive goal strategy, work toward each of your goals, regularly revisit your goals list, assess your progress, adjust your goals and actions, and accomplish all you can.

The fact is, people don't usually set goals unless they're taught to, and most parents and teachers don't teach children the value of setting goals, much less explain how or why goals are important. And usually when people hear about setting goals and giving goals a deadline, when they start working toward the goal and an obstacle gets in the way, many who are new to goals think that working on them is simply too hard. They don't bother with goals, because they don't like running into obstacles and feeling that they have failed at their goal. Ironically, there are just as many obstacles and challenges for people who don't have goals and just go wherever life takes them. Then they get caught up in just trying to exist.

If living day to day without any major goals means you're going to be confronted by obstacles anyway, then you ought to go ahead and set your goals. If you're going to have challenges, you should at least have a reason for them!

If living day to day without any major goals means you're going to be confronted by obstacles anyway, then you ought to go ahead and set your goals.

If you lack vision in your life and you haven't established goals and a plan for your life, when you experience obstacles, they will discourage you even more. What's especially discouraging is that regularly experiencing obstacles without even having the clarity and motivation that comes from purpose, breeds a negative attitude. People can easily fall into the trap of adopting the old, here we go again attitude—bad things always happen to me.

POWER TIP

The nervous system can't tell the difference between imagination and reality. So, imagine more!

But with vision, a goal-setting mentality, a degree of self-mastery, and a never give up mind-set, we begin to understand that obstacles are a necessary part of our life, and they frequently even have a purpose. The purpose may be to teach us a lesson or possibly nothing more than to make us appreciate achieving our goal and overcoming the challenge. Nevertheless, our perception of problems, obstacles, or challenges takes on a whole new meaning when we have a goal. Oh, it doesn't mean that we aren't bothered by the trouble of these obstacles, but we understand that with goals and visions we must often travel an uncharted course. Uncharted courses are bound to bring unexpected challenges. It's something we should come to expect. I know you've heard, "The best-laid plans of mice and men often go awry."

Our perception of problems, obstacles, or challenges takes on a whole new meaning when we have a goal.

Compare that with people who just exist. They are not focused on an outcome, so when problems do arise, there is no purpose moving them to solve their challenge. They have no drive to master their circumstances and avoid letting circumstances control them. Without the purpose of goals, the autopilot in their mind will rarely lead them to the thought: Let's solve this problem. More often their lack of purpose leads them to think, *Woe is me.*

Earlier in the book I told you about a gentleman who bought an old derelict hotel. Remember, it was stone's throw away from an international airport? Remember that the property had sat vacant for an extended period and no one in the hotel industry would touch it? There were certainly challenges in making a hotel property prosperous in spite of the judgment of everyone else in the hotel industry. Even though he was new to the hotel business, the developer didn't let things like other people's opinions rent space in his head. He had a goal and overcame his challenges.

Maybe you're thinking this story is a quaint tale of some little beachside inn and a proprietor who was a one-hit-wonder. That couldn't be farther from the truth. The man who purchased the hotel by the airport is the Honorable Gordon "Butch" Stewart. His name may not ring a bell to you, but his hotels should. His properties comprise the world's number one all-inclusive resort, and they have held that distinction for over a decade. Sandals Resorts and Beaches Resorts are among the most recognized tropical paradise destinations in the world. Butch, as his friends call him, has become one of the world's most successful hoteliers. His privately owned company boasts more than 20 first-class resorts in the Caribbean. Some properties are valued at over $100 million dollars. His resorts are in Jamaica, Turks & Caicos Islands, Antigua, the Bahamas, and St. Lucia. And there's no sign of slowing down. His resorts, his organization, his influence on the region and the world are all simply amazing. Butch Stewart's vision and his clarity of purpose allowed him to make decisions and overcome obstacles and truly energize his life and the lives of everyone he meets. He has mastered energizing life in spite of the obstacles.

When we've developed the mind-set not to let people or our own negative thoughts rent space in our heads, we can move forward with conviction. Our minds think in terms of alternate possibilities. When others think your ideas are off the wall, you think of them as normal and possible. You begin living in a world with practically limitless possibilities, a world that offers incredible options, a world that others just can't see.

When we've developed the mind-set not to let people or our own negative thoughts rent space in our heads, we can move forward with conviction.

I have the opportunity to spend time with Butch from time to time. When you watch someone at his level, when you can see how he works and conducts business, it becomes evident that after many years of not allowing others or things to rent space in his head, he has developed a phenomenal amount of confidence, confidence based on his track record of successes. People at this level have the ability to regularly begin new ventures. That almost goes without saying. But Butch (and a few others like him) can invent new ways of doing things, see new opportunities for success, that no one has ever thought of before. They have no doubt in their own ability to turn ideas into reality, despite what obstacles come in their way.

You begin living in a world with practically limitless possibilities.

One thing I've found in spending time with very successful business people, those who make hundreds of millions and even billions, is that they all have a tremendous amount of confidence. They are the epitome of confidence. With this confidence comes a natural wall of protection that prevents other things from renting space in their heads. This confidence comes from regularly adding to their page 3 in the Four-Step Process. They have an abundance of New Positive Feelings and Experiences. When you have nothing on your page 3, then your confidence is easily shaken. As you have new ideas and share them with others, you can become too easily influenced by what others think and say. This lack of confidence will cause you to be wishy-washy. Always, remember, if you are wishy-washy in your thinking, you will be wishy-washy in your results.

Another great example of energizing your life in spite of the obstacles is Sir Richard Branson. He certainly has well-earned confidence and a proven track record in business and as a globe-trotting adventurer. He's made a considerable investment in commercial space travel. If you've followed any of his adventures, it's obvious this ballooning, aqua-car-driving billionaire doesn't take himself too seriously and seems to have a sense of fun in everything he does. He even bought six space ships. How in the world could someone do that if he let others rent space in his head?

Sir Richard Branson even bought six space ships. How in the world could someone do that if he let others rent space in his head?

The ability to create visions and make them happen as Butch and Richard have done doesn't happen overnight. To many observers, who look at what shining stars like these have accomplished in business, it's mind-blowing and overwhelming. That assessment is certainly understandable. These gentlemen do billions in business each year. Their individual net worth is beyond most people's frame of reference. If you ask most people, "Could you be like either of these successful people?" most would have a hard time picturing it because they see where they personally are right now, and where Branson and Stewart are. There is a massive gap between the two lifestyles.

Their individual net worth is beyond most people's frame of reference. If you ask most people, "Could you be like either of these successful people?" most would have a hard time picturing it.

But allowing that mental gap to get in your way is tantamount to selling yourself short. That's because you're looking at the end, not the beginning. Here is what I mean. If all you had were a basement and a computer and you were asked to type a student magazine for your school, could you do that? I think most of us could manage that. For that matter, if we are no good at typing or writing, we could just convince a fellow student to help us. Seems pretty easy.

How about this scenario? Could you sell air conditioners? Okay, some people who lack confidence in sales are doubting themselves, so let me make it a little more appealing. Could you sell air conditioners if you lived on small, tropical island that got very hot during the day and very few residences or businesses had air conditioners? If you were one of the few people that had air conditioners to sell, do you think that would be an easier sales position?

Richard Branson's first venture was putting together a student magazine in his basement. Butch Stewart sold air conditioners on the island of Jamaica. He was one of the first to offer them. When I ask people if they think they could develop a student newspaper or sell air conditioners on a Caribbean island, most people can get their minds around that. Yet there's a tremendous difference between these starter businesses and the conglomerates developed by each of these entrepreneurs. The distance between these two points is 30 years of independent thought and decision making, 30 years of believing in themselves and their goals, 30 years of not letting others rent space in their heads.

If you chip away at anything for 30 years, you are bound to have some degree of success (though most will not reach billionaire status). We often look at the success of others, and all we see is where they are now. I can promise you that when Richard Branson was making student magazines in his basement he wasn't thinking, *One day I am going to own an airline, have an incredibly successful music label, and buy a few space ships.* One thing leads to another.

You need to keep several things in mind as you develop your big-picture view. First, there will always be unexpected challenges. Deal with them and move on. Second, it always takes longer than you think it should to reach the really big goals and often even the little ones. Don't let your calendar turn into a roadblock. Adjust your plan and move on. Third, look at the whole process as a journey. If you tie your satisfaction to the journey rather than a particular goal, practically everything about your life will be better. Finally, don't let anything outside your own good judgment influence you to give up your goal. Take advice. Listen to advisors with experience. Avoid irrational optimism. Then move forward with your plans. Don't let others rent space in your head.

Don't let anything outside your own good judgment influence you to give up your goal.

When Richard Branson was asked, "How do you cope when things don't go your way?" He responded, "Whenever I experience any kind of setbacks, I always pick myself up and try again. I prepare myself to have another stab at things, with the knowledge I've gained from the previous failure." (Yes, he uses the word "failure.") He continued, "My mother always taught me never to look back in regret, but to move on to the next thing. The amount of time that people waste on failures, rather than putting that energy into another project, always amazes me. I have fun running the Virgin businesses, so a setback is never a bad experience, just a learning curve."

How about Butch Stewart? I can't image him in his early career, while he was personally installing air conditioners in people's homes thinking, *I am going to own the world's most successful all-inclusive hotels and have my own yachts and private jets.*

Success takes time, and this is one more reason we have to make it a journey not a destination. You shouldn't get caught up in thinking you need 30 years. And don't worry that you're starting too late either. Colonel Sanders, founder of the KFC restaurant chain, started his venture after his retirement. The point we must keep in mind is that it takes time, but you have to start somewhere. Now is as good a time as any.

It may sound trite, but it's true that if they can do it, you can too. You might not think you can be where Branson and Stewart are, but you can start with the same humble beginning each of them did. George Harrison initially didn't write any of the Beatles songs, he just played and sang. John Lennon and Paul McCartney were writing all the songs in the early days and George said, "If they can do it, so can I." George started writing and made millions more.

WHO WANTS TO BE A BILLIONAIRE?

Most people would at least admit they would enjoy the financial benefits of being at the level of Branson and Stewart—the jets, yachts and exotic vacations. By no means am I suggesting that everyone who reads this book should make it a goal to be a billionaire. I personally *don't* have a goal to be a billionaire. I know the price they have to pay to reach that level, and I am not willing to pay that price. In spite of that, I have high goals for myself, and I am especially interested in what enables these billionaires to get to these heights without letting other people or things rent space in their heads. With this understanding, I know what I am able to accomplish professionally, and I can take my business and personal life to the level I wish. I can accomplish whatever I want as long as my plan works within my values and beliefs, and those of my family. You can certainly do the same.

I personally **don't** *have a goal to be a billionaire. I know the price they have to pay to reach that level.*

If you are able to develop the mind-set of the people you've just read about, you can chart your own course and determine where you want to be in your personal and professional life. That's control. That's exciting.

SUMMARY

▌ Just because you know how to overcome what's been holding you back so far, that doesn't mean everything will be smooth sailing from here forward.

▌ Setting and achieving goals and constantly trying to refresh your view of your journey will keep you sharp and moving in the right direction.

▌ Simply choosing to take control of their life is something 98 percent of people miss out on.

▌ Even if no one has accomplished what you want to do, that doesn't mean it can't be done. You could be the first.

Chapter 19

"Fill Your Own Well So Your Cup Can Run Over to Help Others"

M ost adults have experienced the joy of giving. It's no secret that it can be incredibly energizing and fulfilling to give to people who are in need or to see a child's eyes light up with absolute joy from a gift.

It's somewhat less obvious that there is far less pleasure and reward from gifts given under duress. I feel bad for people who give because of guilt and not because they simply want to give. It's exactly the same action, but because of the negative feelings associated with it, the payoff, the joy of giving is absent.

I encourage you to give what you can, when you can, because of the mind-set it will create within you. Now, I'm not one of those people who thinks, *All your dreams will come true if you simply believe.* That's ridiculous. Ironically, though, I am convinced that believing very strongly in something will help you have the mind-set to manifest what you believe. With a little adjustment, the previous statement is far more accurate. I am convinced that if you believe in some goal and you are willing to work toward that goal and you take advantage of circumstances which are consistent with that goal, it's very likely you can reach almost any goal you desire.

This second statement is less elegant, but it's far more accurate. If your goal is to share or contribute to others, you can develop ways to make it happen.

Most people would agree that it's important and fulfilling to help others. We do seem to get more enjoyment out of giving when we help someone and expect nothing back. Yet in spite of the fact that we get something back, we should also recognize that there is a cost to giving. This is what makes it so challenging to take the time and justify the cost to help others. It truly does cost us to help people. It may cost you in your time, money, emotions, or some combination of these resources.

We do seem to get more enjoyment out of giving when we help someone and expect nothing back.

Have you ever tried to help someone who seemed to be very depressed and discouraged? If you aren't careful, those emotions can rub off on you. You will actually start taking on some of their emotions. That is a cost to you. Obviously, if you give away money or possessions, there's a cost to you in dollars. If you give up your time, then that's time you can't spend on other things, which are valuable to you and need your personal attention.

Assuming you agree that it's important to give to others, you should include resource recovery as part of your giving plan.

If you're talking about giving money away, you won't be able to help others for very long if you end up homeless. That goes without saying. Yet I regularly see situations where people give away more than they can afford to give because they feel guilty for having what someone else considers too much.

Most people would consider airplane ownership extravagant. In fact, I know people who would suggest that I should sell my airplane and give the money to charity. That's an incredibly short-sighted view. First of all, if I didn't love flying and wasn't driven to acquire a plane and a helicopter, I wouldn't have worked so hard. What's more, I am occasionally able to fly special needs children and their family members, at no cost to them, to various places for medical treatment through the Angel Flight program. I could never help these people unless I had a sufficiently large plane and the budget for travel. I can continue to contribute to charities and help deserving families only as long as I keep my own financial resources in line.

I know people who would suggest that I should sell my airplane and give the money to charity. That's an incredibly short-sighted view.

The same is true for emotional giving. If you share the gift of personal, emotional investment with people in need, you must consider that you will need to recharge your own batteries. Some people recharge their emotional batteries by focusing on uplifting, positive things in their life, which helps them feel good enough to get in the emotional trenches with someone in need.

So if giving away money or property means that you must have a plan for earning more to care for yourself and future charitable efforts, and if giving of yourself emotionally requires that you do things to enrich yourself emotionally, then how can you create more time so that you have time you can give to others? Strictly speaking, you can't create more time. All you can do is rearrange your priorities and devote more or less time to various activities.

Since most people understand that you have to make money to be able to give it away, I'd like to focus on the other resources involved in giving. I believe that you need to be a bit selfish in order to be a good giver.

I really like what self-made billionaire Oprah Winfrey has to say about the subject, "Fill your own well so your cup can run over to help others."

POWER TIP

We are the sum total of everything we have ever experienced from birth till now.

When you consider that statement, it's incredibly powerful. It especially means a lot to self-starter and accomplishment-oriented personalities. Motivation to keep pushing yourself to the next level remains as strong as ever when your giving is motivated by desire rather than guilt. When people are motivated by achieving goals and they recognize the benefits of helping others, they are naturally moved to accomplish in order to improve their own position *and* in order to share their benefits. It creates a win-win situation. But keep in mind that this applies to more than money.

If you don't do things that enrich you, motivate you, and repay you, while you give away your resources, you will eventually be spent in every sense of the word.

I know parents of large families who do absolutely everything they can and sacrifice personal pleasures and rewards in order to be there full-time for their family and especially for the kids. The problem in this scenario is that the giving parent(s) don't correlate their contribution to their family with resources that have to be replenished. Maybe they look at their efforts as their job or duty, but if they could just figure out some way to refill their own resources, they would have even more to give to their family and not feel so depleted at the end of every day. Unfortunately, they feel guilty if they allow themselves to take time off from the kids or the office to refresh their mind and soul. But a live parent is better than a dead one. A live manager is better than a dead one.

If you don't do things that enrich you, motivate you, and repay you, while you give away your resources, you will eventually be spent in every sense of the word.

When we allow our lives to get this hectic and don't regain control, we are that much more susceptible to all kinds of negative influences. Before long there will be all kinds of stuff renting space in our heads, and we won't have the energy to evict the unwelcome intruders.

So if you agree that you need to fill your own well first, do you know how? You should. If you want to keep enjoying the benefits of giving you must pace yourself. Pacing yourself does two things. One, it makes us stop and smell the flowers along the way. Occasionally, slowing down a bit or relaxing is a reward in and of itself. And second, getting away from those things that tap our resources refuels us to keep helping others without feeling so drained. It lets us have more so we can give more.

Mastering the balance between giving and refueling gives you longevity in what you do and keeps you from burning out, plus you'll have a much more fulfilling life.

Mastering the balance between giving and refueling gives you longevity in what you do and keeps you from burning out.

Be on the lookout for ways you can fill your own well every day, week, month, and year. For example, I do specific things every day that keep my well full. Each day before going to work, I try to do some reading. What refills my well daily more than anything is the drive to my office. When I'm driving, I don't drive with the radio on. I need complete silence. It's my think time. I'm constantly around people in my office, or I'm conducting a seminar, doing an interview, or coaching someone. I love being around people and helping people, but the entrepreneur part of my personality needs to be replenished too. Having quiet time on a regular basis does wonders for me. It mentally recharges my batteries, and it doesn't cost me anything financially.

What about you? Maybe you get recharged with a walk or some exercise. Maybe you're refreshed by reading the newspaper on your patio while having a cup of coffee. Do whatever charges your batteries so you have energy to give to others.

Once you understand what energizes you, fill your well. Remember this isn't something we are only doing just for ourselves. Our motive here isn't to simply fill our own well. We want to fill our well so that we are able to help others. Enrich yourself so you can enrich the lives of others.

Once you understand what energizes you, fill your well.

Admittedly, those who have more are able to give more. America's nineteenth-century industrialist, Andrew Carnegie, could have been this country's first billionaire. Instead, he gave away 90 percent of his fortune over a period of 18 years. When his secretary warned him that he was depleting his personal capital, he happily replied, "Delighted to hear it my boy, keep it up." That same era saw John D. Rockefeller, one of the richest men in the world, give away $750 million in his lifetime.

Enrich yourself so you can enrich the lives of others.

You've just read an entire book about accomplishment, overcoming obstacles, and getting to the next level in your own life. You now have insights into those who have accomplished incredible feats, and you have a host of tools you can use in your struggle to overcome your own challenges. I assure you that you'll benefit even more if you share your journey to the next level by helping people in need along the way. So live richly and give richly, fill your own well so your cup can run over to help others.

SUMMARY

- One of the true joys on your path should be giving.
- Do well, accomplish things, reach goals, and give to others.
- Don't give because you think you'll get it back. Sometimes you do, sometimes you don't. Give because it's the right thing to do.
- Giving keeps things in perspective.
- If you are achievement-oriented, it is likely that you are motivated by reaching personal, business, and spiritual goals and by acquiring certain possessions. You should never give away all you've worked for because that takes away your motivation and you're through.
- On the other hand, you should always give away something of your accomplishments and share your wealth with others as you go.
- I assure you that you'll benefit even more if you share your journey to the next level by helping people in need along the way.
- *Live richly and give richly, fill your own well so your cup can run over to help others!*

Index

Acknowledgment, important to change, 41–52
American Idol example of irrational optimism, 63–64, 69
Attitude:
 negative thinking and, 112, 127–129
 positive thinking and, 80–85, 89–90
Attitude Adjusting Statements, 85, 141–145
Awareness, increasing of, 8

Bagley, Dan, 223
Banister, Roger, 15
"Begin with the end in mind" concept, 157–158
Beliefs:
 derived from life's experiences, 31–34
 to handle mental vertigo, 99–101
 intellectualized versus internalized, 43–44
 replacing old with new, 34–39
"Be on stage" concept, 214–217
"Be prepared" concept, 111–116
Bowling example of irrational optimism, 62–63
Branson, Richard, 15–16, 247–248, 250

Carnegie, Andrew, 258
Change:
 importance of acknowledgment to, 41–52
 need to embrace, 34, 35
Cigarette smokers example of lack of acknowledgment, 49–50
Cold-calling, feelings about, 207–208
Confidence, source of, 247

DEA agents story, 231–237
Denial, as hindrance to change, 42, 44–45
Discouragement, as result of positive thinking, 76–77
Distinctions, importance of recognizing, 59–60

Emotions:
 in conflict with goals, 29, 178–180, 182–183, 203–204
 control of, 80–85, 158–159, 217–218
 creating positive, in Four-Step Process, 186–188
 identifying and interpreting negative, 200–202, 205
 identifying and using productive, 150–156, 205–206
 keeping journal of, 193–194
 as last to change, 26, 180–182
 mental vertigo and, 97
 power of, 191–200
 range of, in adults, 152
 steps to control of, 206–211
Employees, who "rent space in your head," 37–38
Empowering thoughts, in Four-Step Process, 173–186, 239
 confirming acceptance of, 182–186
 emotions and, 178–182
 imagination versus reality, 175–178
 logic and, 174–175
Excuses, about lack of success, 104–105
Experiences:
 creating positive, in Four-Step Process, 186–188
 as influence on behavior, 31–39

Feelings. *See* Emotions
Flying:
    in example of mental vertigo,
      93–101
    negative thoughts and planning
      for, 140–141
    simulator training and, 112–116
Four-Step Process, 161–190
    sample pages for recording of,
      165–168
    Step 1, answering "Why must I
      change this behavior?", 163,
      169–170
    Step 2, listing limiting beliefs,
      170–173
    Step 3, listing empowering
      beliefs or thoughts, 173–186,
      239
    Step 4, creating new positive
      emotions and experiences,
      186–188
Friends, irrational optimism and, 69
Frustration, using positively,
    152–153

Games, playing with your mind,
    213–219
Gardener, Carol, 58
Getty, J. P., 222–223
Giving, joy of, 253–259
Goals. *See also* Success
    achieving despite obstacles,
      243–252
    being realistic about, 64–72
    costs of achieving, 44, 66–68, 224
    emotions and, 156, 178–180,
      182–183, 203–206
    happiness and, 221–228
    planning and, 108–110

Habits, time required to change,
    185
Happiness, goals and, 221–228
Harrison, George, 250
Helicopter example of
    acknowledgment, 46–48
Hope, 74, 85–89

Hotel business story, 16–18, 245–246
How to Get Rich (Trump), 120

Imagination, reality and, 175–178,
    206
Influences, negative. *See* "Rent
    space in your head"
Insurance, as good use of negative
    thoughts, 126–127
Irrational optimism:
    distinguishing from optimism,
      59–61
    need for alternative plan and,
      65–66
    realistic goals and, 64–72
    recognizing, 61–64

Journal, keeping record of emotions
    in, 193–194
Journey, acknowledging life as,
    221–228
Joy of giving, 253–259

Kennedy, John F., Jr., 93, 97

Lemons and lemonade. *See* Moving
    on
Life:
    acknowledging as journey,
      221–228
    re-editing "video" of, 229–242
Limiting beliefs:
    emotional reaction and, 202
    listing, in Four-Step Process,
      170–173
    using logic to overcome,
      174–176
Logic, to change limiting beliefs,
    174–176
Lying to self:
    to begin to fool the brain, 177–180
    positive thinking and, 147–150,
      154–155

Maltz, Maxwell, 175
Marathon race story, success and,
    106–110

Medical treatment, need for, 154, 201

Mental vertigo, 93–102
  beliefs and, 99–101
  flying and, 93–101

Mentors, 69–70

Micromanagers, 38

Mind games, 213–219

Motivation, need for more than, 1–12

Moving on:
  helping someone with, 57–58
  taking time before, 53–56

National Enquirer, 27

Negative emotions, 6–8. *See also* Negative thinking
  identifying and interpreting, 200–202, 205
  learning to control, 80–85
  productive use of, 193–194

Negative experiences:
  perceptions and, 131–146
  writing about, to learn from, 50–51

Negative thinking, 13–21, 111–130. *See also* Four-Step Process
  analysis of, 116–119
  attitude and, 112, 127–129
  positive results from, 37, 111–116, 122–129, 141–142
  refusing to reward, 19
  responding to others', 142–145
  unbalanced view of, 119–122

Noise, example of changing perceptions about, 16–18

"No problem" statement, 175–177

Objections, planning to overcome, 116–119

Obstacles:
  achieving goals despite, 243–252
  persevering despite, 1–3

Optimism. *See* Irrational optimism

Pain, focus on future, as motivation, 194–200

Parents, irrational optimism and, 69

Perception, 131–146, 163
  changing of one's, 135–145

Personal achievement, understanding process of, 9

Personal timing, moving on and, 53–58

Personal tragedy, getting over, 23–30, 53–58

Phobias, overcoming. *See* Four-Step Process

Planning:
  benefit of negative thoughts to, 116–119
  mentors and optimism, 69–70

Positive thinking, 73–91, 147–160
  attitude and, 80–85, 89–90
  emotions and useful, 150–156
  as end in itself, 5
  in Four-Step Process, 186–188
  hope and, 74, 85–89
  often not useful, 10, 19, 73–77, 147–150
  techniques for using, 157–159
  time and, 20, 77–80

Problems. *See* Obstacles

Procrastination, 44, 194–196

Professional help, need for, 154, 201

Programming, by life's experiences, 31–39

Psycho-Cybernetics (Maltz), 175–177

Reality, imagination and, 175–178, 206

"Refueling," personal, 255–259

"Rent space in your head," explained, 13–21

Responsibility, for quitting or continuing, 46–50

Reticular activating system, 8

Rewiring your brain. *See* Four-Step Process

Risk taking, rule of, 14–15

Rockefeller, John D., 258

Secrets That My Millionaire Mentors Taught Me About Business and Success (CD series), 106
Simulator flight training, 112–116
Software company training story, 42–43
Steps. *See* Four-Step Process
Stewart, Gordon "Butch," 16–18, 245–247, 249, 250
Stories, not enough to change lives, 3–4
Success:
    excuses made about lack of, 104–105
    not easy or painless, 103–110
    time required for, 249–250

Time and timing:
    moving on and, 53–58

new habits and, 185
positive thinking and, 20, 77–80
success and, 249–250
Tough love, example of, 32–33
Tragedy, getting over, 23–30, 53–58
Trump, Donald, 120

Vertigo. *See* Mental vertigo
"Video of life," re-editing of, 229–242

Wants, of most people, 9
"Why," asking:
    about negative emotions, 6–8
    in Four-Step Process, 163, 169–170
Winfrey, Oprah, 256